# The Ultimate Guide to SAT® Grammar Workbook

# 3rd Edition

Erica L. Meltzer

Test directions reprinted by permission of the College Board. The SAT® is a trademark registered by the College Board, which was not involved in the production of this material and does not endorse this product.

ISBN-13: 978-1518794100
ISBN 10: 1518794106

# Table of Contents

# Test 1 Answer Sheet

1. Ⓐ Ⓑ Ⓒ Ⓓ
2. Ⓐ Ⓑ Ⓒ Ⓓ
3. Ⓐ Ⓑ Ⓒ Ⓓ
4. Ⓐ Ⓑ Ⓒ Ⓓ
5. Ⓐ Ⓑ Ⓒ Ⓓ
6. Ⓐ Ⓑ Ⓒ Ⓓ
7. Ⓐ Ⓑ Ⓒ Ⓓ
8. Ⓐ Ⓑ Ⓒ Ⓓ
9. Ⓐ Ⓑ Ⓒ Ⓓ
10. Ⓐ Ⓑ Ⓒ Ⓓ
11. Ⓐ Ⓑ Ⓒ Ⓓ
12. Ⓐ Ⓑ Ⓒ Ⓓ
13. Ⓐ Ⓑ Ⓒ Ⓓ
14. Ⓐ Ⓑ Ⓒ Ⓓ
15. Ⓐ Ⓑ Ⓒ Ⓓ
16. Ⓐ Ⓑ Ⓒ Ⓓ
17. Ⓐ Ⓑ Ⓒ Ⓓ
18. Ⓐ Ⓑ Ⓒ Ⓓ
19. Ⓐ Ⓑ Ⓒ Ⓓ
20. Ⓐ Ⓑ Ⓒ Ⓓ
21. Ⓐ Ⓑ Ⓒ Ⓓ
22. Ⓐ Ⓑ Ⓒ Ⓓ

23. Ⓐ Ⓑ Ⓒ Ⓓ
24. Ⓐ Ⓑ Ⓒ Ⓓ
25. Ⓐ Ⓑ Ⓒ Ⓓ
26. Ⓐ Ⓑ Ⓒ Ⓓ
27. Ⓐ Ⓑ Ⓒ Ⓓ
28. Ⓐ Ⓑ Ⓒ Ⓓ
29. Ⓐ Ⓑ Ⓒ Ⓓ
30. Ⓐ Ⓑ Ⓒ Ⓓ
31. Ⓐ Ⓑ Ⓒ Ⓓ
32. Ⓐ Ⓑ Ⓒ Ⓓ
33. Ⓐ Ⓑ Ⓒ Ⓓ
34. Ⓐ Ⓑ Ⓒ Ⓓ
35. Ⓐ Ⓑ Ⓒ Ⓓ
36. Ⓐ Ⓑ Ⓒ Ⓓ
37. Ⓐ Ⓑ Ⓒ Ⓓ
38. Ⓐ Ⓑ Ⓒ Ⓓ
39. Ⓐ Ⓑ Ⓒ Ⓓ
40. Ⓐ Ⓑ Ⓒ Ⓓ
41. Ⓐ Ⓑ Ⓒ Ⓓ
42. Ⓐ Ⓑ Ⓒ Ⓓ
43. Ⓐ Ⓑ Ⓒ Ⓓ
44. Ⓐ Ⓑ Ⓒ Ⓓ

# Writing and Language Test
## 35 MINUTES, 44 QUESTIONS

**Turn to Section 2 of your answer sheet to answer the questions in this section.**

## DIRECTIONS

Each passage below is accompanied by a number of questions. For some questions, you will consider how the passage might be revised to improve the expression of ideas. For other questions, you will consider how the passage might be edited to correct errors in sentence structure, usage, or punctuation. A passage or a question may be accompanied by one or more graphics (such as a table or graph) that you will consider as you make revising and editing decisions.

Some questions will direct you to an underlined portion of a passage. Other questions will direct you to a location in a passage or ask you to think about the passage as a whole.

After reading each passage, choose the answer to each question that most effectively improves the quality of writing in the passage or that makes the passage conform to the conventions of standard written English. Many questions include a "NO CHANGE" option Choose that option if you think the best choice is to leave the relevant portion of the passage as it is.

**Questions 1-11 are based on the following passage and supplemental information.**

**The People's Bank**

Born in 1940, Muhammad Yunus is a social **1** entrepreneur; banker, economist and civil leader who was awarded the Nobel Peace Prize for pioneering the concepts of microcredit and microfinance.

In 1974, Yunus, who was then working as a professor at Chittagong University in **2** Bangladesh, and took his students on a field trip to a poor village. There, he interviewed a woman who made bamboo stools. The woman explained that she had to borrow money to buy raw

**1**

A) NO CHANGE
B) entrepreneur; banker; economist, and
C) entrepreneur, banker, economist, and
D) entrepreneur, banker, economist and,

**2**

A) NO CHANGE
B) Bangladesh, and he took
C) Bangladesh, taking
D) Bangladesh, took

bamboo for each stool. After repaying her loans, sometimes at rates as high as 10% per week, she was barely able to **3** roll a profit. As a result, she struggled to feed both herself and her children. Were the woman able to borrow money with lower rates of **4** interest, Yunus recognized, she would likely be able to amass an economic cushion and rise above subsistence level.

Yunus decided to take matters into his own hands. **5** He personally lent the equivalent of a few dollars to 42 basket-weavers in the village. He discovered that the tiny loans not only helped the basket weavers survive **6** and also creating the motivation for them to pull themselves out of poverty. Against the advice of banks and the government, he continued to distribute what he termed "micro-loans."

**3**

A) NO CHANGE
B) flip
C) count
D) turn

**4**

A) NO CHANGE
B) interest; Yunus recognized
C) interest, and Yunus recognized
D) interested, Yunus recognizing

**5**

Which choice most effectively supports the information that follows?

A) NO CHANGE
B) In 1965, Yunus received a Fulbright fellowship to study in the United States.
C) Traditional banks did not want to make low-interest loans to the poor because of high risk of default.
D) During that time, he set up a packaging factory, which became very profitable.

**6**

A) NO CHANGE
B) and creating
C) but also to create
D) but also created

**7** In 1971, Yunus founded a citizen's committee along with other Bangladeshis in the United States. In 1983, he made funds available by forming the Grameen Bank. Ron Grzywinski and Mary Houghton of ShoreBank, a community development bank in Chicago, helped Yunus with the official incorporation under a grant from the Ford Foundation. The Bank provides loans to entrepreneurs who are unable to qualify for traditional bank loans. "Grameen bank" means "village bank," and it is founded on the **8** principles in trust and solidarity.

**7**

Which choice provides the most effective introduction to the paragraph?

A) NO CHANGE
B) Yunus has served on the Global Commission of Women's Health and the UN Expert Group on Women and Finance.
C) As a student at Chittagong College, Yunus had studied drama as well as economics.
D) Yunus reasoned that if basic financial resources could be made widely available, then economic wonders could occur

**8**

A) NO CHANGE
B) principles of
C) principals in
D) principals of

The Grameen Bank not only reversed conventional banking practice but it also created a cost effective weapon to fight poverty, giving people access to funds that would otherwise have remained outside their reach. **9** Membership grew dramatically throughout the 1980s and 1990s, although it began to decline around 2000. The Bank has also served as a catalyst in the overall development of socio-economic conditions of the poor, particularly women. **10** Nevertheless, 97% of Grameen borrowers are women, and over 97% of the loans are paid back in full – a recovery rate **11** higher than any other banking system.

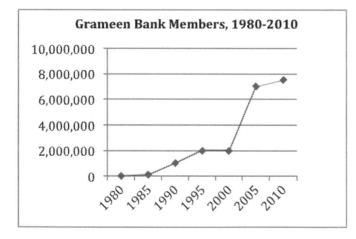

**Grameen Bank Members, 1980-2010**

**9**

Which choice most accurately and effectively represents the information in the graph?

A) NO CHANGE
B) Membership grew dramatically between 1980 and 1985 before leveling off.
C) Membership grew slowly until 2000, after which it increased dramatically.
D) Membership increased steadily until 2005 and then leveled off.

**10**

A) NO CHANGE
B) Therefore,
C) However,
D) DELETE the underlined word.

**11**

A) NO CHANGE
B) higher then any other banking system.
C) higher than the rate of any other banking system.
D) higher then the rate of any other banking system.

**Questions 12-22 are based on the following passage.**

**Everyday Art**

— 1 —

For more than a quarter of a century, artist Gabriel Orozco (b. 1962) has **12** forged a career marked by constant surprise and innovation, blurring the boundaries between art and reality. Orozco resists confinement to a single medium in order to engage **13** they're imaginations. He roams freely among drawing, photography, sculpture, installation, and painting. Basing his work on a series of recurring themes and techniques, Orozco **14** divides his time between Mexico City, New York, and France. One work might consist of exquisite drawings scribbled on airplane boarding passes; another could involve sculptures made from recovered trash. His exploration of such varied materials allows audiences to investigate **15** associations between objects that are hidden.

**12**

A) NO CHANGE
B) derived
C) fabricated
D) claimed

**13**

A) NO CHANGE
B) their imaginations.
C) you're imagination.
D) viewers' imaginations.

**14**

Which choice most effectively sets up the examples that follow?

A) NO CHANGE
B) has exhibited his work in art galleries on every continent except Antarctica.
C) uses urban landscapes and common objects to erase the line between art and the everyday environment.
D) has received numerous awards, including a DAAD artist-in-residence grant to work in Berlin.

**15**

A) NO CHANGE
B) hidden associations between objects.
C) associations hidden between objects.
D) associations that are hidden between objects.

— 2 —

Orozco's nomadic lifestyle began to strongly inform his work around this time. **16** Once, while wandering through a small town in Brazil, Orozco spotted some oranges left over from a market, positioned one on each of several tables, and photographed them. Unlike many mainstream artists, who often oversaw huge studios with many assistants and elaborate production techniques, Orozco also worked **17** by himself in solitude or with a single assistant. He therefore remains free to create art where and when he chose.

— 3 —

Orozco was born in 1962 in Veracruz, Mexico. His father, Mario Orozco Rivera, was a mural painter and art professor at the University of Veracruz. When Orozco was six, the family relocated to Mexico City so that his father could work on various mural commissions. **18** Orozco often accompanied his father to mural sites and museum exhibitions. He overheard many conversations about art and politics.

**16**

The writer is considering deleting the underlined sentence. Should the sentence be kept or deleted?

A) Kept, because it illustrates how Orozco's preference for wandering influenced his art.

B) Kept, because it explains why Orozco became interested in photography.

C) Deleted, because it is inconsistent with the paragraph's focus on Orozco's studio.

D) Deleted, because it implies that Orozco rejected all forms of mainstream art.

**17**

A) NO CHANGE

B) in solitude

C) by himself in a solitary way

D) alone by his solitary self

**18**

In context, which choice best combines the underlined sentences?

A) While Orozco often accompanied to his father to mural sites and museum exhibitions, he overheard many conversations about art and politics.

B) Orozco, who often accompanied to his father to mural sites and museum exhibitions, overhearing many conversations about art and politics.

C) Orozco often accompanied to his father to mural sites and museum exhibitions, where he overheard many conversations about art and politics.

D) Orozco often accompanied to his father to mural sites and museum exhibitions, and that was where he overheard many conversations about art and politics.

— 4 —

In 1981, Orozco entered the National School of Fine Arts in Mexico City, but he found the curriculum conservative **19** and the work uninteresting. When a friend invited him to study in Spain, he eagerly accepted. In 1986, he enrolled at Madrid's **20** Circulo de Artes; one of the leading art schools in Spain. It was there that his instructors introduced him to a broad range of contemporary artists working in non-traditional formats.

— 5 —

Orozco then returned to Mexico, where he began to collaborate with other artists, including Damián Ortega, Gabriel Kuri, and Abraham Cruzvillegas. The group **21** hung out once a week for five years, and Orozco's home became a place where many artistic and cultural projects took shape. In the early 1990s, however, Orozco relocated once again, this time to New York. He also began to spend increasing amounts of time in Paris.

— 6 —

Although Orozco has exhibited in works around the world and won dozens of awards, he considers his art a process of continuous exploration. Combining his passion for life with the poetry of chance encounters, Orozco's work offers a distinctive model for the ways in which artists can affect the world with their work.

**Question 22 asks about the previous passage as a whole.**

**19**
A) NO CHANGE
B) and the work being uninteresting.
C) the work was uninteresting.
D) and the work was uninteresting also.

**20**
A) NO CHANGE
B) Circulo de Artes. One
C) Circulo de Artes: one
D) Circulo de Artes, it was one

**21**
A) NO CHANGE
B) convened
C) met
D) chilled together

**Think about the passage as a whole as you answer question 22.**

**22**
To make the passage most logical, paragraph 2 should be placed

A) where it is now.
B) after paragraph 3.
C) after paragraph 4.
D) after paragraph 5.

**Questions 23-33 are based on the following passage.**

**A Library for New York**

The origins of the New York Public Library date back to the time when New York was emerging as one of the world's largest cities. By the second half of the nineteenth century, New York City's population had **23** increased the population of Paris, which was then around 2.5 million. Among **24** they're inhabitants was former governor Samuel J. Tilden (1814-1886), who left the majority of his fortune to "establish and maintain a free library and reading room in the city of New York."

By the 1890s, New York had two major libraries – the Astor and the Lenox – but neither of them **25** was a truly public institution, and both were experiencing financial difficulties. John Bigelow, a New York attorney and trustee of Tilden's estate, **26** devised a plan to combine the resources of the two existing libraries into a new entity that would be known as The New York Public Library. The library would be located on the site of the Croton Reservoir, **27** a popular strolling place that occupied two blocks of Midtown Manhattan. The plan, signed and agreed upon on May 23, 1895, was praised as an unprecedented example of private philanthropy for the public good.

**23**

A) NO CHANGE
B) surpassed
C) outdone
D) enlarged

**24**

A) NO CHANGE
B) their
C) it's
D) its

**25**

A) NO CHANGE
B) were
C) is
D) are

**26**

A) NO CHANGE
B) threw together
C) whipped up
D) mentally cogitated

**27**

The writer is considering deleting the underlined phrase (placing a period after the word *Reservoir*). Should the phrase be deleted?

A) Yes, because the library could no longer serve as a strolling place.
B) Yes, because it digresses from the passage's focus on the New York Public Library.
C) No, because it provides information about the size and location of the new library.
D) No, because it indicates the role of private philanthropy in the library's construction.

John Billings, one of the most renowned librarians of his day, was appointed director of the library, and he had a lofty vision for the new building. It called **28** on an enormous reading room set on top of seven floors of stacks as well as the country's most rapid book delivery system. Billings' design, first **29** sketched on a scrap of paper, eventually became the blueprint for the structure. Some of the city's most prominent architectural firms competed to build the library, and **30** the winning design featured a pair of lions flanking the main entryway. The result was the largest marble structure ever attempted in the United States. Before construction on the library itself could begin, however, **31** the books from the Lenox and Astor Libraries were consolidated into a single collection. Finally, the site was cleared, and the cornerstone for the library was laid in May 1902.

**28**

A) NO CHANGE
B) to
C) for
D) about

**29**

A) NO CHANGE
B) sketched on a scrap of paper –
C) sketched, on a scrap of paper,
D) sketched on a scrap of paper;

**30**

Which choice most logically completes the sentence while reinforcing its main point?

A) NO CHANGE
B) it was funded with a mix of private and public donations.
C) the library now consists of research and circulating collections.
D) the renowned firm of Carrère & Hastings was selected to design and construct it.

**31**

Which choice provides the most effective transition to the information that follows?

A) NO CHANGE
B) workers had to spend two years dismantling the reservoir.
C) famed author Washington Irving was chosen to serve as President of the library's Board of Trustees.
D) the library hired nationally prominent experts to oversee its collections.

Work progressed slowly but steadily on the monumental structure. During the summer of 1905, huge columns were put into place, and work on the roof started. By the end of 1906, work on the interior rooms **32** begins. Four years later, 75 miles of shelves were installed to house the immense collections. More than one million books were set in place for the official dedication on May 23, 1911. The next day, the library officially **33** opened its doors at precisely 9:08 in the morning, the first patron filed a slip to request a book, receiving it only six minutes later.

**32**

A) NO CHANGE
B) has begun.
C) had begun.
D) will begin.

**33**

A) NO CHANGE
B) opened its doors. At precisely 9:08 in the morning,
C) opened its doors, at precisely 9:08 in the morning,
D) opened its doors at precisely 9:08 in the morning

**Questions 34-44 are based on the following passage.**

**Designing the Web**

As we point and click our way through a website, most of us don't stop to think about how that site came to exist. Websites don't just **34** appear, though they must be carefully created and maintained by web designers, whose jobs require a synthesis of technical and creative skills. **35** However, web designers must not only be familiar with the most common programming languages such as html and Javascript but they must also have a thorough knowledge of color and design principles.

Most new businesses will need to have a website designed in order to market their services to potential customers. Some companies will want a bright, modern look with flashy graphics, while others **36** will prefer to interview a number of designers. Either way, a designer is necessary to ensure that the site looks professional and is easy for users to navigate.

**34**

A) NO CHANGE
B) appear, though,
C) appear though,
D) appear, though;

**35**

A) NO CHANGE
B) Meanwhile,
C) In contrast,
D) In fact,

**36**

Which choice most effectively sets up the contrast in the sentence?

A) NO CHANGE
B) will have a more limited budget.
C) will choose from existing templates.
D) will want to project a more subdued image.

Business owners may locate a web designer by doing an Internet search or by asking friends and colleagues for recommendations. When a business owner finds a **37** perspective designer, the two will usually meet to discuss what information the site should include and develop a "site map" – a chart indicating how the site will be laid out. They will discuss the number of pages that are necessary as well as **38** the colors, fonts, and graphics that will be used.

Then, the web designer will work independently to produce a sample site, and the business owner will provide feedback. Sometimes, a final product is achieved quickly; **39** therefore, many drafts are necessary before everyone is satisfied.

**37**

A) NO CHANGE
B) perspective designer –
C) prospective designer,
D) prospective designer;

**38**

Which choice gives a second supporting example that is most similar to the example already in the sentence?

A) NO CHANGE
B) the products and services that the business provides.
C) the types of customers the business serves.
D) the programming language the designer will use.

**39**

A) NO CHANGE
B) ironically,
C) in other instances,
D) likewise,

While no particular degree or program of study is required to become a website designer, many designers **40** holding undergraduate or graduate degrees in artistic fields such as graphic design or technical fields such as computer science. Some web designers, however, are self-taught. **41** Web design is a field in which talent and attention to detail **42** are usually considered more important than academic diplomas.

**40**

A) NO CHANGE
B) hold
C) held
D) would hold

**41**

The writer is considering adding the following sentence.

> Workers in this category may initially pursue web design as a hobby, only later realizing that they can transform their skills into a career.

Should the writer make this addition?

A) Yes, because it supports the idea that web design is a creative field.
B) Yes, because it provides additional relevant about self-taught web designers.
C) No, because it detracts from the paragraph's focus on the types of degrees web designers hold.
D) No, because it suggests that web design does not require a specific set of skills.

**42**

A) NO CHANGE
B) is
C) was
D) being

Regardless of background, web designers must demonstrate flexibility. Although some designers are employed by companies, most work on a project-to-project **43** basis, each project takes anywhere from several weeks to several months. Long hours may sometimes be necessary, **44** especially when a designer must juggle multiple projects and manage competing deadlines. On the other hand, web designers often have far more scheduling flexibility than employees in other fields. And with the Internet playing an increasingly important role in most industries, good web designers are always in high demand.

**43**

A) NO CHANGE
B) basis. Each project taking
C) basis; and each project takes
D) basis, with each project taking

**44**

The writer is considering deleting the underlined portion of the sentence (replacing the comma after "necessary" with a period.) Should it be kept or deleted?

A) Kept, because it explains why web designers must sometimes work long hours.
B) Kept, because it clarifies the role that web designers play within companies.
C) Deleted, because the passage indicates that many web designers are self-employed.
D) Deleted, because it detracts from the paragraph's focus on web designers' flexibility.

**Test 1: Explanations**

1. C: Commas with list

When separating items in a list, either commas or semicolons should be used consistently; the two should not be mixed and matched. A and B can thus be eliminated. D is incorrect because a comma should not be placed between *and* and the last item in a list. That leaves C, which correctly uses a comma to separate the items in the list.

2. D: Non-essential clause

The key to answering this question is to back up to the beginning of the sentence and recognize that the commas around the phrase *who was then working as a professor at Chittagong University in Bangladesh* signal a non-essential clause. If the phrase is crossed out of the sentence, what remains is not a grammatical construction: *Yunus...and took students on a field trip to a poor village*. The simplest way to correct the sentence is to replace the gerund *taking* with the conjugated verb *take*. That makes the answer D.

3. D: Idiom

The correct idiomatic phrase is "turn a profit."

4. A: Non-essential clause

Although the placement of the non-essential clause may sound odd to you, the sentence makes perfect sense when the clause is removed: *Were the woman able to borrow money with lower rates of interest...she would likely be able to amass an economic cushion and rise about subsistence level.* The commas around the phrase are therefore correct. B incorrectly places a semicolon between a dependent clause (*Were the woman able to borrow money with lower rates of interest*) and an independent clause (*she would likely be able to amass an economic cushion and rise above subsistence level*); C is wrong for the same essential reason as B: "comma + and" is grammatically identical to a semicolon. D is incorrect because the gerund *recognizing* creates a fragment.

5. A: Add/delete/change

The previous sentence states that *Yunus decided to take matters into his own hands*, with the word *matters* referring to the village woman's inability to earn a living wage from selling brooms. The sentence in question should thus indicate what Yunus did to help. In addition, the following sentence refers to *the tiny loans*, so the sentence in question should logically introduce the idea of the loans. Both A and C contain the idea of lending, but only A explains what Yunus did to help the villagers. C focuses on the banks, not on Yunus.

6. D: Word pair, parallel structure

Because *not only* appears earlier in the sentence, *but also* must appear in the underlined portion. That eliminates A and B. The underlined phrase must also be parallel to the construction after *not only*. What appears after *not only*? A verb in the past tense (*helped*). Only D contains that construction, so it is correct.

7. D: Add/delete/change

Start by ignoring the first sentence, and consider the rest of the paragraph. In particular, focus on the second sentence since the topic sentence must directly introduce it. What does the rest of the paragraph talk about? The formation of the Grameen Bank. The second sentence indicates that Yunus *made funds available*. Logically, the topic sentence must be connected to finance or money. The original version is unrelated to either of those things and can thus be eliminated immediately. Although C mentions economics, this answer is completely off-topic and can be eliminated as well. B indicates that Yunus is considered an expert in finance, but it is not directly related to Yunus's founding of the Grameen Bank. D is correct because it logically describes Yunus's reasoning for starting the bank.

8. B: Diction; idiom

Principal = most important; principle = rule. That narrows it down to A and B. The correct idiom is "principles of," making B correct.

## 9. C: Graph

The graph indicates that initial bank membership increased slowly in the 1980s and 1990s, then shot way up beginning in the early 2000s before slowing again. No declines in membership are indicated, so A can be eliminated immediately. B states the opposite of the graph: membership increased *slowly* in the 1980s and 1990s. Be careful with D: membership did increase until 2005, but it did not increase *steadily*; the graph reveals a very large and abrupt jump. C is correct because that jump did in fact occur around 2000.

## 10. D: Transition

*Nevertheless* and *however* both indicate a contrasting relationship, so you can start out by assuming that both answers are wrong. No question can have more than one correct answer, so if two answers have the same meaning, both can be eliminated. Now back up and consider the relationship of the sentence in question to the previous sentence. The previous sentence indicates that the Grameen Bank has helped poor women develop economically, and the sentence in question describes the bank's focus on and success in helping women. Those are similar ideas, but the second is not actually the result of the first, as *therefore* would imply. No transition is required, making D correct.

## 11. C: Faulty comparison, diction

The sentence incorrectly compares a recovery rate to a banking system. In order for the sentence to be correct, a recovery rate must be compared to a recovery rate. Only C and D do so, but D is incorrect because *than*, not *then*, should be used to form comparisons.

## 12. A: Diction

In this case, *forge* is used idiomatically to mean "build" or "create." It has nothing to do with falsifying. The other words do not make sense in context.

## 13. D: Pronoun agreement, apostrophes

A is incorrect because you would not say "…in order to engage they are imaginations." In addition, *they're* should not be used before a noun. C is wrong for the same reason. You're = you are, and you would not say "…in order to engage you are imaginations." Even though B supplies a correctly formed possessive pronoun, that answer is incorrect because the sentence never specifies whom *their* refers to. Only D solves the problem entirely by supplying a noun that indicates exactly whose imaginations are inspired by Orozco's works.

## 14. C: Add/delete/change

The question asks you to identify which choice most effectively sets up the information that follows, so start by reading *after* the underlined portion. If you focus on the sentence in which it appears, you might get sidetracked. The following sentence indicates that Orozco creates art out of things like boarding passes and trash – not typical art materials. The correct answer must therefore be related to that idea, and C is the only option that matches. All of the other answers relate to the international character of Orozco's career – a theme that is strongly present in the passage but that does not correspond to the sentences following the underlined portion.

## 15. B: Misplaced modifier

The original version as well as C and D imply that the objects themselves are hidden, whereas the sentence means to say that the *associations* between objects are hidden. B is the only option that makes the correct meaning clear.

## 16. A: Add/delete/change

When you are asked to consider whether a sentence should be added or deleted, make sure you start by reading it in context, paying particular attention to the topic sentence. Without that information, it will be difficult to tell whether the sentence is on- or off-topic. In this case, the topic sentence indicates that Orozco's art was shaped by his *nomadic lifestyle*. The underlined sentence refers back to that idea with the phrase *preference for wandering* (a nomad is someone who wanders), then provides a specific of example of a work that Orozco created while wandering. The original sentence does therefore support the main idea of the paragraph, making the answer A.

17. B: Redundancy, shorter is better

*By himself, alone*, and *in solitude* all have the same meaning. Only one of these words/phrases should therefore be used.

18. C: Combining sentences

Since the sentences themselves don't provide any overwhelmingly obvious clues about how they should be combined, you can start by checking the answers. The two sentences do not have a contrasting relationship, as the contradictor *while* implies, so **A** is incorrect. To check **B**, cross out the non-essential clause: *Orozco…overhearing many conversations about art and politics*. No, that's a fragment. C correctly places a comma between an independent clause and a dependent clause, and appropriately uses *where* to refer to a place. If you're not sure, however, check D. That answer is grammatically acceptable but unnecessarily wordy (*and that was where he overheard…*). When two answers are both grammatically correct and have the same meaning, the shorter one will usually be right. That is the case here, making C correct.

19. A: Parallel structure

Although the construction in the original version may sound odd to you, it is in fact acceptable. The verb *found* "applies" to both *the curriculum* and *the work*, and it is not necessary to place another verb before *uninteresting*. The gerund *being* in B creates an awkward, ungrammatical construction and usually signals a wrong answer. C works just fine on its own but not when it is plugged into the sentence (*he found the curriculum conservative the work uninteresting*). D creates a run-on: a comma must be placed before *and* because the transition is used to separate two independent clauses. In addition, the use of *also* at the end of the sentence is unnecessarily awkward.

20. C: Commas, colons

Since a semicolon and a period are identical, A and B can be eliminated immediately. (Both periods and semicolons should only be placed between two complete sentences, but here they are placed between a sentence and a fragment.) In D, the construction "comma + it" signals a commas splice: two complete sentences incorrectly separated by a comma. C is correct because a colon must come after a full sentence but can come before a fragment. The information after the colon is also correctly used to explain what the Circulo de Artes was.

21. C: Register

*Hung out* and *chilled together* are both far too casual, and *convened* is too formal. *Met* correctly maintains the moderately serious tone of the passage.

22. D: Paragraph order

Start by looking at the first sentence of paragraph 2, since it must logically follow the end of the paragraph that correctly precedes it. The words *around this time* are key. Logically, the end of the previous paragraph must indicate when "this time" was. The end of paragraph 1 makes no mention of a time, however, eliminating A. Likewise, the ends of paragraphs 3 and 4 make no mention of specific times either. Paragraph 5, however, does mention 1990 in the last sentence. It also indicates that Orozco moved around a lot. That is consistent with the reference to Orozco's *nomadic lifestyle* in paragraph 2, so the paragraph belongs after paragraph 5.

23. B: Diction, idiom

Logically, the sentence is trying to convey that New York's population became larger than Paris's population. In that context, the correct verb is *surpassed*. None of the other options is idiomatically acceptable.

**24. D: Pronoun agreement, apostrophes**

Answer this question in two parts. First, you would not say "Among they are inhabitants," so A is clearly wrong. Likewise, you would not say "Among it is inhabitants," eliminating C as well. Now, what noun does the underlined pronoun refer to (whose inhabitants)? New York. Cities are singular, so the singular pronoun its is required.

**25. A: Subject-verb agreement, tense**

Neither = neither one = singular. That eliminates B and D. The date 1890 indicates that the past tense is required, making was correct.

**26. A: Register**

Threw together and whipped up are both far too casual, and mentally cogitated is too formal. Devised means "thought up" and is idiomatically correct as well as consistent with the passage's moderately serious tone.

**27. C: Add/delete/change**

If the underlined phrase were deleted, the sentence would still make sense, but an important piece of contextual information would be lost. Most readers would simply have no idea where the Croton Reservoir was or how large a space it occupied. The underlined phrase should therefore remain, and the answer is C. D is completely off-topic – the size and location of the reservoir had nothing to do with private philanthropy (donations).

**28. C: Preposition, idiom**

Call for is an idiomatic phrase meaning "require" or "request." That is the only logical meaning in this context.

**29. A: Non-essential clause**

The key to this question is to consider the whole sentence, not just the underlined portion. If you back up to the beginning of the sentence, you'll find that the comma after design marks the beginning of a non-essential clause (first sketched on a scrap of paper) that can be crossed out of the

sentence without affecting its general meaning (Billings' design...eventually became the blueprint for the structure). Since a comma is used to mark the beginning of the non-essential clause, a comma must be used to mark the end as well. That eliminates B and D. C is incorrect because no comma should be used before a preposition (on).

**30. D: Add/delete/change**

What does the beginning of the sentence indicate? That prominent firms competed to build the library. The correct answer must therefore be consistent with that idea. D is the only answer that mentions a well-known ("renowned") architectural firm; it is therefore correct.

**31. B: Add/delete/change**

What does the information following the underlined portion indicate? That construction did not begin until the lot was cleared. Furthermore, the word finally implies that clearing the site took a long time. B is the only answer consistent with that idea – the phrase two years corresponds to the idea that construction could not begin for an extended period. The other options have nothing to do with preparing for the physical construction of the building.

**32. C: Tense**

The dates 1905 and 1906 clearly indicate that the correct answer must be in the simple past tense. A is in the present, and D is in the future, so both can be eliminated immediately. B is incorrect because the present perfect (has begun) is used only for actions continuing into the present, and the passage is clearly talking about events that began and ended in the past.

**33. B: Combining and separating sentences**

This question has the potential to be tricky if you don't read all the way to the end of the sentence. If you do, you're likely to notice that it's way too long. In fact, the sentence is really two sentences stuck together. If the comma after morning were replaced with a period, the sentences would be divided effectively, but unfortunately that's not an option. The key is to recognize that although the phrase *at precisely 9:08 in the morning* makes sense at the end of the first sentence, it also fits at the beginning of the second sentence. B is therefore correct. C creates a comma splice by placing a comma rather than a period between the two sentences, and D creates the same problem as the original version.

## 34. D: Non-essential clause, comma splice

Although the sentence is grammatically acceptable the way the original version is written, it does not actually make sense – the information after the comma expands on the information before the comma, and *though* is used to signal a contradiction. B is incorrect because *though* cannot be used non-essentially here. If it is crossed out, a run-on sentence is created. C creates a comma splice, as suggested by the construction "comma + they." D correctly the two sentences with a semicolon, placing *though* at the end of the first sentence. That placement eliminates the need for the sentences to convey contrasting ideas and solves the problem that is created in A.

## 35. D: Transition

Because the question asks about a transition at the beginning of a sentence, you must back up and read the previous sentence in order to determine the correct relationship. What does the previous sentence indicate? That web design requires both technical and creative skills. What does the sentence begun by the underlined transition indicate? That designers must understand both programming languages and design principles. So the sentences express similar ideas. That eliminates both A and C. *Meanwhile* is normally used to emphasize that one event happened at the same time as another event, and it simply doesn't make sense here. That leaves D, which correctly indicates that the sentences express similar ideas.

## 36. D: Add/delete/change

The question asks you to focus on the contrast in the sentence, so start by reading the first half. Since it refers to *flashy graphics*, the correct answer must indicate the opposite. *Subdued* is the opposite of *flashy*, so D is correct.

## 37. C: Diction, comma

Perspective = point of view; prospective = potential. Only the second meaning makes sense in this context, eliminating A and B. D is incorrect because a semicolon should only be used between two complete sentences, and the phrase before the semicolon would be a fragment.

## 38. A: Add/delete/change

The non-underlined example (*number of pages*) consists of basic practical information necessary to create a website. It also supports the previous sentences, which indicate that business owners and website designers discuss how sites are *laid out*. The correct answer must therefore be related to site layout. If you recognize that A fits, you can choose it and move on. Otherwise, play process of elimination. While B refers to important information that would presumably be featured on a business website, products and services are not key components of a website *layout*. Likewise, customers are an important part of a business, but they are not as directly relevant to laying out a website as are colors and graphics. In D, a programming language is certainly necessary to create a website, but it is not basic, practical information like the number of pages.

## 39. C: Transition

Since the transition is the first word of the clause, back up and read the first half of the sentence to determine the relationship. What does it say? That sometimes things get done quickly. What does the sentence in question say? Sometimes things take a long time. So there is a contrasting relationship. Only C fits.

## 40. B: Sentence vs. fragment

The gerund *holding* in the original version creates a fragment; the easiest way to correct the sentence is to conjugate the verb by removing the –ING. That gives you B. Both C and D are incorrect because the surrounding verbs (*is, are*) are all in the present, and there is no reason to switch tenses.

### 41. B: Add/delete/change

Start by considering the context. The paragraph as a whole discusses what sort of training web designers need, and the previous sentence specifically mentions self-taught designers. The sentence to be added is therefore consistent with the focus of the paragraph and, most importantly, with the sentence that immediately precedes it. Furthermore, it provides more information about just what sort of people are likely to transition into a career in web design without formal training. Although the paragraph does indicate that web designers can come from artistic backgrounds, there is nothing in the sentence itself that specifically supports the idea that web design is creative. The answer is therefore B.

### 42. A: Subject-verb agreement

Don't be fooled by the answers in different tenses. The fact that there are both singular and plural options tells you that the question is testing agreement. The subject of the underlined verb is *talent <u>and</u> attention to detail* – two things. A plural verb is therefore required, making *are* the only option.

### 43. D: Comma splice

Remember that "comma + pronoun" usually signals a comma splice, and *each* is a pronoun. That makes A incorrect. B is incorrect because the gerund *taking* creates a fragment, and semicolons should only be placed between two complete sentences. C is incorrect because a semicolon should be placed before *and*. D correctly uses the construction "with … -ing" to join the final clause to the rest of the sentence smoothly.

### 44. A: Add/delete/change

Start by reading the entire sentence that contains the underlined phrase – that's the most important piece of context. Now, what role does the underlined information play in that sentence? It explains/gives more specific information about when web designers must work long hours. Is that information relevant to the sentence? Yes. So it should be kept, and the answer is A.

# Test 2 Answer Sheet

1. Ⓐ Ⓑ Ⓒ Ⓓ
2. Ⓐ Ⓑ Ⓒ Ⓓ
3. Ⓐ Ⓑ Ⓒ Ⓓ
4. Ⓐ Ⓑ Ⓒ Ⓓ
5. Ⓐ Ⓑ Ⓒ Ⓓ
6. Ⓐ Ⓑ Ⓒ Ⓓ
7. Ⓐ Ⓑ Ⓒ Ⓓ
8. Ⓐ Ⓑ Ⓒ Ⓓ
9. Ⓐ Ⓑ Ⓒ Ⓓ
10. Ⓐ Ⓑ Ⓒ Ⓓ
11. Ⓐ Ⓑ Ⓒ Ⓓ
12. Ⓐ Ⓑ Ⓒ Ⓓ
13. Ⓐ Ⓑ Ⓒ Ⓓ
14. Ⓐ Ⓑ Ⓒ Ⓓ
15. Ⓐ Ⓑ Ⓒ Ⓓ
16. Ⓐ Ⓑ Ⓒ Ⓓ
17. Ⓐ Ⓑ Ⓒ Ⓓ
18. Ⓐ Ⓑ Ⓒ Ⓓ
19. Ⓐ Ⓑ Ⓒ Ⓓ
20. Ⓐ Ⓑ Ⓒ Ⓓ
21. Ⓐ Ⓑ Ⓒ Ⓓ
22. Ⓐ Ⓑ Ⓒ Ⓓ

23. Ⓐ Ⓑ Ⓒ Ⓓ
24. Ⓐ Ⓑ Ⓒ Ⓓ
25. Ⓐ Ⓑ Ⓒ Ⓓ
26. Ⓐ Ⓑ Ⓒ Ⓓ
27. Ⓐ Ⓑ Ⓒ Ⓓ
28. Ⓐ Ⓑ Ⓒ Ⓓ
29. Ⓐ Ⓑ Ⓒ Ⓓ
30. Ⓐ Ⓑ Ⓒ Ⓓ
31. Ⓐ Ⓑ Ⓒ Ⓓ
32. Ⓐ Ⓑ Ⓒ Ⓓ
33. Ⓐ Ⓑ Ⓒ Ⓓ
34. Ⓐ Ⓑ Ⓒ Ⓓ
35. Ⓐ Ⓑ Ⓒ Ⓓ
36. Ⓐ Ⓑ Ⓒ Ⓓ
37. Ⓐ Ⓑ Ⓒ Ⓓ
38. Ⓐ Ⓑ Ⓒ Ⓓ
39. Ⓐ Ⓑ Ⓒ Ⓓ
40. Ⓐ Ⓑ Ⓒ Ⓓ
41. Ⓐ Ⓑ Ⓒ Ⓓ
42. Ⓐ Ⓑ Ⓒ Ⓓ
43. Ⓐ Ⓑ Ⓒ Ⓓ
44. Ⓐ Ⓑ Ⓒ Ⓓ

# Writing and Language Test
## 35 MINUTES, 44 QUESTIONS

**Turn to Section 2 of your answer sheet to answer the questions in this section.**

---

**DIRECTIONS**

Each passage below is accompanied by a number of questions. For some questions, you will consider how the passage might be revised to improve the expression of ideas. For other questions, you will consider how the passage might be edited to correct errors in sentence structure, usage, or punctuation. A passage or a question may be accompanied by one or more graphics (such as a table or graph) that you will consider as you make revising and editing decisions.

Some questions will direct you to an underlined portion of a passage. Other questions will direct you to a location in a passage or ask you to think about the passage as a whole.

After reading each passage, choose the answer to each question that most effectively improves the quality of writing in the passage or that makes the passage conform to the conventions of standard written English. Many questions include a "NO CHANGE" option. Choose that option if you think the best choice is to leave the relevant portion of the passage as it is.

---

**Questions 1-11 are based on the following passage and supplemental information.**

**Space Project**

An enormous metallic dome sits in the middle of a laboratory floor as workers look on from the balconies above. Two figures clad in orange help a third one secure an inflatable spacesuit and helmet. **1** In front of a blackboard, a man stands holds a model space shuttle. These are all images captured by photographer Vincent Fournier in the series *Space Project*, which reflects its creator's fascination with the space age.

**1**

Which choice most closely matches the stylistic pattern established earlier in the paragraph?

A) NO CHANGE
B) Holding a model space shuttle, a man stands in front of a space shuttle.
C) A man holding a model space shuttle stands in front of a blackboard.
D) Standing in front of a blackboard, a man holds a model space shuttle.

As a child, Fournier was captivated by movies such as *2001: A Space Odyssey*, but these days he's not interested in space in the traditional sense. **2** However, he can't be caught outside, pointing his camera to the night sky. His real interest is the people who study the universe: the astronomers, astronauts, and space enthusiasts **3** whom dream about launching away from the earth and setting off to visit other worlds. For years Fournier has traveled the globe, creating an immense body of images documenting the people who commit their lives to understanding the universe at large.

**4** Fournier was inspired to create *Space Project* after a visit to an observatory in Hawaii prompted him to think about space exploration. Initially, though, he wasn't sure what form the project would take. After several months of research, he decided to base it on the book, *From Earth to the Moon* by Jules Verne. Written in 1865, it tells the story of an attempt to launch three people into orbit in a projectile, with the goal of landing on the moon.

**5** Although the book was written nearly a century before the first space shuttle was launched, it captures **6** a prolonging curiosity about the universe that began long before such a voyage was possible.

**2**

A) NO CHANGE
B) Next,
C) For example
D) Otherwise,

**3**

A) NO CHANGE
B) who dream
C) which dream
D) and dream

**4**

Which choice provides the most appropriate introduction to the paragraph?

A) NO CHANGE
B) Fournier must wait for up to a year to gain access to some locations.
C) Initially, Fournier financed his work with money from his commercial work.
D) Fournier's background in advertising has helped him stage photographs effectively.

**5**

A) NO CHANGE
B) Since
C) Despite
D) Because

**6**

A) NO CHANGE
B) an accelerating
C) an extending
D) an enduring

Fournier's project is a study in contrasts, combining a historic documentation of space exploration with **7** detailed images. On one hand, the project is a photographic archive of the most important space organizations in the world: the Mars Desert Research Station in Utah, Gagarine Cosmonaut Training Center near Moscow, observatories in the Chilean desert, and the Guyana Space Center in Kourou, French Guiana. On the other hand, Fournier also includes staged and electronically edited photographs. In one image, for instance, astronauts climb peaks in a barren, red valley – perhaps one located on Mars. In another, **8** a figure clutching a spacesuit helmet stands in a futuristic room.

**7**

Which choice most effectively sets up the contrast in the sentence and is most logical with the information in the rest of the paragraph?

A) NO CHANGE
B) imaginary scenes.
C) depictions of the natural world.
D) authentic photographs.

**8**

Which choice gives a second supporting example that is most similar to the example in the previous sentence?

A) NO CHANGE
B) a series of buildings rise out of a snowy landscape.
C) a planet surrounded by rings gleams brightly against a dark backdrop.
D) a group of scientists observe a creature that is half-insect and half-machine.

According to Fournier, *Space Project* is inspired by the elements of mystery and wonder **9** that draw people to study space. As children, we look at the stars and suddenly realize that we are only a tiny part of an infinite universe. **10** Fournier's photographs give a sense of the finished and unfinished, the immenseness of time and space. They are about the unseen, the mystery of space travel, and the universe around us. They leave us with a sense of both awe and comfort, **11** even if we are part of both the sky and the Earth.

**9**

A) NO CHANGE
B) that draws
C) that has drawn
D) which draws

**10**

The writer is considering adding the following sentence.

> Scientists have discovered that the universe is expanding at an increasing rate.

Should the writer make this addition?

A) Yes, because it supports the idea that the universe is a vast place.
B) Yes, because it explains why people find space so mysterious.
C) No, because it interrupts the paragraph's focus on the inspiration behind Fournier's work.
D) No, because the paragraph is written from the point of view of an artist rather than a scientist.

**11**

A) NO CHANGE
B) although
C) as if
D) when

**Questions 12-22 are based on the following passage.**

**Reducing Airplane Noise**

It is difficult to imagine that a park landscape could owe its existence to the noise made by airplanes during takeoff and landing, but that is exactly the case at the Buitenschot Land Art Park. The park, which is located just past the edge of the Polderban runway at Schiphol airport in **12** Amsterdam, and it consists of a series of interlocking hedges and ditches laid out in a diamond pattern. Spread across 80 acres of green space, it contains many typical park elements, such as bicycle paths and **13** furrowed ridges. It's real purpose, however, is to keep the surrounding area quiet.

Schiphol airport is one of the busiest airports in the world, with more than 1600 flights **14** passing through each day. In 2003, the Polderban runway – the airport's longest – was constructed. Its outlying location was originally intended to reduce the overall noise disturbance by redirecting air traffic over areas with a lower population **15** density instead, it created another problem: ground-level noise. As soon as the runway was finished, residents of the neighborhoods around the airport began to complain about the **16** incessant low-frequency drone that was constantly present.

**12**

A) NO CHANGE
B) Amsterdam, consisting
C) Amsterdam, consists
D) Amsterdam – consists

**13**

Which choice gives a second supporting example that is most similar to the example already in the sentence?

A) NO CHANGE
B) sports fields.
C) valleys.
D) open farmland.

**14**

A) NO CHANGE
B) whooshing by
C) barging in
D) zooming around

**15**

A) NO CHANGE
B) density, instead
C) density. Instead,
D) density instead

**16**

A) NO CHANGE
B) incessant low-frequency drone.
C) incessant low-frequency drone that would not stop.
D) incessant and constant low-frequency drone.

The site on which Schiphol is located was once the bed of an enormous lake, and it was originally chosen because it contained the sort of **17** flat, open, terrain that is ideal for landing airplanes. Unfortunately, the qualities that made the area so well-suited to being an airport also turned it into a giant megaphone. **18** The problem was further **19** aggravated by the unique properties of ground waves. Unlike other types of sound waves, ground waves are not easily deflected by traditional sound barriers such as concrete walls; the low frequency, long wavelength sound skips over them. Airport officials were forced to find another way to divert the noise.

**17**

A) NO CHANGE
B) flat, open terrain –
C) flat, open terrain,
D) flat, open terrain

**18**

The writer is considering adding the following sentence.

> Even a person speaking at normal volume could be heard dozens of yards away.

Should the writer make this addition?

A) Yes, because it provides support for an idea introduced in the previous sentence.
B) Yes, because it explains how low-frequency sound waves are amplified.
C) No, because it adds an irrelevant detail focus on the types of degrees web designers hold.
D) No, because the passages focuses on the noise made by airplanes.

**19**

A) NO CHANGE
B) exceeded
C) overloaded
D) irritated

In 2008, the Netherlands Organization for Applied Scientific Research [TNO] was brought in to conduct a study. Researchers discovered that noise levels decreased significantly in the fall, just after the surrounding fields had been plowed. **20** Until the resulting ridges in the land deflected the sound away from the ground, the researchers concluded that the most effective way to solve the airport's problem would be to make that feature of the landscape permanent. Artist Paul De Kort was hired to design the park; he used GPS to plow 150 perfectly straight and symmetrical furrows with six foot high ridges between them. The park, which officially opened in October 2013, makes use of meticulous yet simple **21** landforms. It creates a landscape that not only serves a specific function but is also an intriguing public space. It has also reduced airport noise **22** slightly, resulting in normal levels throughout the entire region.

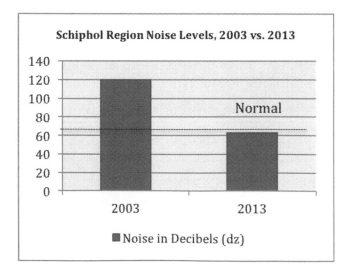

**20**

A) NO CHANGE
B) While the resulting ridges
C) Because the resulting ridges
D) The underlined ridges

**21**

In context, which choice best combines the sentences at the underlined portion?

A) landforms, and a landscape is created by it that not only serves
B) landforms, creating a landscape that not only serves
C) landforms, this creates a landscape that not only serves
D) landforms and creating a landscape that not only serves

**22**

Which choice offers an accurate interpretation of the information in the graph?

A) NO CHANGE
B) by more than half, although levels are still above normal
C) by around half, resulting in approximately normal levels
D) by around half, resulting in significantly below normal levels

**Questions 23-33 are based on the following passage.**

**Preserving the Past**

Digital archivists are responsible for overseeing and collecting historically significant documents and other forms of **23** media, including: photographs, film clips, maps, and audio recordings. Some digital archivists are employed at public institutions such as community libraries or government agencies; others are affiliated with private organizations such as museums, universities, or historical societies. Regardless of where **24** he or she works, digital archivists must possess in-depth knowledge of both current and historical affairs in order to determine which images or documents are worthy of preservation.

In addition to documenting national and international gatherings, **25** digital archivists collaborate closely with other workers. When a city or town holds a parade, for instance, many different photographs of the event are sent to newspapers in the area. A few of the photographs appear **26** their, but a number of additional photos that do not appear are kept as well. It is the job of digital archivists to sort through dozens or even hundreds of images and decide which ones should be retained and which ones can be discarded. **27** The selected images are then scanned and tagged so that they can be easily located in the future.

**23**

A) NO CHANGE
B) media, including photographs, film clips, maps,
C) media; including photographs, film clips, maps,
D) media, including photographs; film clips, maps

**24**

A) NO CHANGE
B) one works,
C) you work,
D) they work,

**25**

Which choice most effectively sets up the information that follows?

A) NO CHANGE
B) digital archivists are responsible for recording local events.
C) digital archivists work extensively with computers.
D) digital archivists handle confidential material.

**26**

A) NO CHANGE
B) around that place
C) in those publications
D) in this

**27**

Which choice best completes the description of the process of preserving images?

A) NO CHANGE
B) Images should be checked for problems once or twice a year.
C) New technologies that make images available to the wider public may be implemented.
D) Archivists well-versed in preserving electronic media are in high demand.

In some cases, digital archivists must also sort through papers and photographs that are decades – or even 28 hundreds, of years old. Because some of these documents are often very fragile and easily ruined, they must be handled with extreme care. In such cases, workers must use special tools to extract the documents from 29 its wrappings in order to ensure that the lighting does not cause fading or other damage.

[1] Digital archivists must also have an in-depth knowledge of industry standards. [2] Specifications are regularly updated to reflect new changes in technology, and archivists must ensure that documents are maintained according to the correct specifications. [3] If images are not preserved properly, parts of them may appear discolored. [4] As result, digital archivists must pay close attention to detail. 30

While the popular image of an archivist is of someone who sits alone in a dark room, shuffling through crumbling papers, archivists' jobs are actually quite varied. In addition to creating and maintaining databases that allow members of the public to locate specific records, 31 they must advise users on how to access, use, and interpret archives. Furthermore, they must produce training materials for new procedures, arrange exhibitions, and supervise less experienced staff members.

**28**

A) NO CHANGE
B) hundreds of years old.
C) hundreds of years, old.
D) hundreds – of years old.

**29**

A) NO CHANGE
B) it's
C) their
D) they're

**30**

The writer is considering adding the following sentence to the paragraph.

They may also become blurry or unfocused.

The best placement for this sentence is

A) before sentence 1.
B) after sentence 2.
C) before sentence 3.
D) before sentence 4.

**31**

A) NO CHANGE
B) thus
C) but
D) and

The Academy of Certified Archivists offers a certification program to archivists. In order to qualify, candidates must complete a Masters degree, pass a written test, and **32** obtaining professional experience. **33** Individuals, who have a graduate diploma in archival studies, must have at least a year of professional experience, while those with a degree in a different field must have at least two years of experience. Archivists can also improve their career prospects by enrolling in continuing education courses and by transferring to larger facilities with a larger number of management positions.

**32**

A) NO CHANGE
B) obtain
C) they obtain
D) will obtain

**33**

A) NO CHANGE
B) Individuals who have a graduate diploma in archival studies
C) Individuals, who have a graduate diploma in archival studies
D) Individuals who have a graduate diploma in archival studies,

**Questions 33-44 are based on the following passage.**

**The First Computer**

Over the last few decades, the power of computers has increased dramatically. In 2000, even powerful computers could not perform as many calculations per second as an insect brain, but scientists project that the average personal computer **34** will reach that milestone by 2020. Growth is projected to continue at a similar rate throughout the twenty-first century. By 2060, a single computer might be able to perform the same number of calculations per second as **35** all human brains.

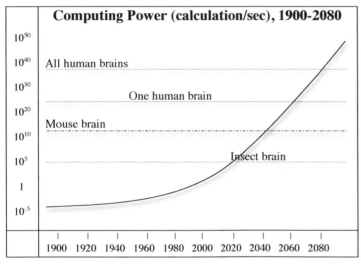

Given these advances, it is easy to forget just how short the history of the computer really is. Ada Lovelace first conceived of an "analytical engine" in the 1840s, but not until a century later **36** did the computer age truly begin.

**34**

Which choice offers an accurate interpretation of the information in the graph?

A) NO CHANGE
B) will surpass that milestone by 2020.
C) will reach that milestone by 2040.
D) will reach that milestone by 2060.

**35**

Which choice offers an accurate interpretation of the information in the graph?

A) NO CHANGE
B) an insect brain.
C) a mouse brain.
D) a human brain.

**36**

A) NO CHANGE
B) does
C) was
D) has

One of the earliest precursors to the modern computer was the ENIAC. Developed in the 1940s by University of Pennsylvania **37** researchers John Mauchley and J. Presper Eckert; the ENIAC was capable of adding 5,000 numbers per second – an amazing feat for a machine of that era. **38** Capable of solving a variety of numerical problems, it weighed thousands of tons and took up nearly 2,000 square feet. It also included dozens of panels, each of which performed a different function. Unfortunately, the computer broke down constantly: at least two or three of its vacuum tubes burned out each day. Finally realizing that the tubes burned out less frequently if the computer was never turned off, **39** the decision was made by engineers to let it run continuously.

**37**

A) NO CHANGE
B) researchers John Mauchley, and J. Presper Eckert,
C) researchers, John Mauchley and J. Presper Eckert
D) researchers John Mauchley and J. Presper Eckert

**38**

Which choice most effectively sets up the information that follows?

A) NO CHANGE
B) Heralded in the press as a "mechanical brain,"
C) With countless vacuum tubes, diodes, and other parts,
D) Thrilling scientists and industrialists,

**39**

A) NO CHANGE
B) the decision being made by engineers to let it run continuously.
C) engineers decided to let it run continuously.
D) it was decided by engineers that it would run continuously.

One of the peculiarities that distinguished ENIAC from all later computers was the way in which instructions were set up on the machine. **40** Thousands of wires had to be plugged for each single instruction of a problem. The process could take weeks. When calculations finally began, a single problem could run for several weeks before a "changeover" occurred. **41** To make stuff go faster, researcher later "microprogrammed" ENIAC's plugboards with a repertoire of 50-100 commonly used instructions.

Which choice most effectively combines the underlined sentences?

A) Thousands of wires had to be plugged for each single instruction of a problem, a process that could take weeks.

B) Thousands of wires had to be plugged for each single instruction of a problem, and this process taking weeks.

C) Thousands of wires had to be plugged for each single instruction of a problem; which could take weeks.

D) Thousands of wires had to be plugged for each single instruction of a problem, this process could take weeks.

Which choice best maintains the tone established in the passage?

A) NO CHANGE
B) To expedite the computations,
C) To hurry the thing up,
D) To speed up the process,

The limitations of the ENIAC were always clear, and in 1944, Eckert and Mauchley began work on a new computer, which became known **42** to be the EDVAC. The EDVAC was a very large machine; **43** nevertheless, it was smaller and more powerful than the ENIAC. It was also much more reliable; ten years after its construction, the EDVAC was still in use. **44** It also made use of binary code, a system of representing text as ones and zeroes that continues to be used to this day.

**42**

A) NO CHANGE
B) for
C) as
D) in

**43**

A) NO CHANGE
B) consequently,
C) as such,
D) likewise,

**44**

The writer wants a conclusion that conveys how the EDVAC had more in common with modern computers than the ENIAC did. Which choice best accomplishes this goal?

A) NO CHANGE
B) Eventually, it was replaced by BRLESC, a first-generation electronic computer.
C) It included a magnetic tape player-recorder as well as a timer and a dispatcher unit that could send instructions to other units.
D) By 1960, EDVAC was running over 20 hours a day, with error-free run time averaging eight hours.

**Test 2: Explanations**

1. C: Parallel structure

The simplest way to approach this question is to look at the beginning of the each of the previous sentences; the correct answer must begin the same way. Sentence 1: *An enormous metallic dome* … Sentence 2: *Two figures*… Both sentences begin with nouns, so sentence 3 must begin with a noun as well. Only C begins with a noun (*A man*), so it is the only possible option.

2. C: Transition

Start by crossing out the existing transition. Then, determine the relationship between the sentence in question and the sentence before it on your own. Sentence 1: Fournier doesn't have a traditional interest in space. Sentence 2: He doesn't spend his time photographing the sky. Even if you can't pinpoint the relationship, you can likely tell that the sentences express similar ideas. *However* and *otherwise* are contradictors, so eliminate A and D. The paragraph isn't listing a sequence of events, so *next* doesn't fit either. That leaves *for example*, which makes sense: the sentence is illustrating the idea that Fournier doesn't demonstrate his interest in space in a traditional way by giving an example of something that he *doesn't* do.

3. B: Who vs. whom

*Who*, not *whom*, should be used before a verb, and *dream* is a verb. C is incorrect because *which* refers to things, not people. D is incorrect because it creates a nonsense construction when plugged back into the sentence.

4. A: Add/delete/change

The information you need to answer the question is located immediately after the topic sentence – in this instance, the latter part of the paragraph doesn't provide much help. What is the focus of the couple of sentence following the topic sentence? The early stages of the project. Logically, then, the topic sentence must be related the project's beginning. Only A fulfills that criterion. The other options are *related* to the project but do not deal specifically with its origins.

5. A: Transition

The contradictor *although* in the original version correctly expresses the contrast between the two parts of the sentence: people couldn't actually travel into space when Jules Verne published *From Earth to the Moon* vs. the possibility of space travel was still fascinating. The only other contradictor is *despite*, and that word creates an ungrammatical construction when it is plugged into the sentence.

6. D: Diction

The phrase *Although the book was written nearly a century before the first space shuttle was launched* indicates that the correct word must mean "lasting a long time." Only *enduring* has that meaning and makes sense in context. Don't get distracted by *prolonging*, which does not have the right connotation: it implies that an event continued after it was supposed to end. *Extending* (stretching out), and *accelerating* (going faster) do not fit.

7. B: Add/delete/change

The original version sounds pretty good in context, so it's crucial to recognize that you're looking for a contrast. What does the sentence indicate Fournier's study combines? A *historic documentation of space exploration with _____.* The underlined portion must therefore refer to the opposite of "historic documentation." The opposite of something that actually happened is something imaginary, and that's what B says. The other options do not create the correct contrast.

8. D: Add/delete/change

Although the question only refers you to the previous sentence, it is also helpful to back up two sentences in order to determine what idea the examples must support (Fournier includes staged and electronically edited photographs). The previous sentence provides an example of a photograph that is clearly staged, so the correct answer must include a staged/edited photograph as well. A, B, and C all refer to images that exist in real life, whereas the half-insect/half-machine image in D could only have been created electronically.

## 9. A: Subject-verb agreement

The subject of the underlined verb is the plural noun *elements*; the singular noun *wonder*, which appears immediately before the verb, is part of the prepositional phrase *of mystery and wonder*, which separates the subject from the verb. A plural verb (*draw*) is therefore required, making the original version the only option. All of the other answers include singular verbs.

## 10. C: Add/delete/change

What is the sentence in question about? The fact that the universe is expanding. What is the paragraph about? The inspiration for and themes of Fournier's *Space Project*. Do those two things go together? No. So A and B are out. Simply put, the sentence is off topic, which is essentially what C says.

## 11. C: Transition

If you have trouble wrapping your head around what the original sentence is trying to say, don't get caught up trying to make sense out of it because it doesn't actually make sense. More effectively, start by crossing out the transition and considering the two parts of the sentence without it. The first part indicates that Fournier's photographs give people *a sense of awe and comfort*, and the second part states that *we are part of both the sky and the Earth*. Even if the exact relationship between those statements isn't clear, they're still expressing ideas that generally go together. *Although* is a contradictor, so B can be eliminated. If you don't recognize that C makes sense in context, check D. *They leave us with a sense of both awe and comfort, <u>when</u> we are part of both the sky and the Earth*. That doesn't really make sense either: *when* implies that Fournier's viewers are actually sometimes part of the sky and the Earth. In contrast, *as if* implies that Fournier's photographs are effective because they leave viewers with the *sense* that they are part of both the sky and the Earth – a much more logical meaning.

## 12. C: Non-essential clause

If you focus only on the underlined portion of the sentence, the original version might seem to make sense; however, if you back up and read the sentence from the beginning, you will see that it contains a non-essential clause (*which is located just past the edge of the Polderban runway at Schiphol airport in Amsterdam*). As a shortcut, know that non-essential clauses are almost always followed by conjugated verbs. That gives you C as the answer right away. Otherwise, cross the non-essential clause out of the sentence: *The runway… and it consists of a series of interlocking hedges and ditches laid out in a diamond pattern*. Clearly, that doesn't work. B also doesn't make sense: the gerund *consisting* turns the sentence into a fragment. D is incorrect because non-essential clauses can be set off by either commas or dashes, but the two cannot be mixed and matched.

## 13. B: Add/delete/change

The existing example is that of a *typical park element*. The correct answer must therefore be a typical park element as well. Only B fits that criterion.

## 14. A: Diction

*Zooming around* and *whooshing by* are both too casual, and *barging in* has the wrong connotation. Only *passing through* conveys the correct meaning using moderately formal vocabulary, so the original version is correct.

## 15. C: Separating sentences

The construction "comma + it" in the original version signals a comma splice. Now, the key to answering the question is to recognize that the sentence in which the underlined phrase appears is actually two sentences, and that the word *Instead* make sense as the beginning of the second sentence. B is incorrect because it creates a comma splice, placing a comma rather than a period between the two sentences; D creates a run-on, placing no punctuation at all between the sentences. Only C correctly places a period between the two sentences.

16. B: Redundancy, shorter is better

*Incessant*, *constant*, and *would not stop* all have the same meaning, so only one of these options should be used.

17. D: Commas with list

The original version is incorrect because no comma should be placed between an adjective and the noun it describes (e.g. *open, terrain*). B is incorrect because there is no reason to break up the sentence with a dash after *terrain*, and no punctuation should normally be used before the word *that*. C is incorrect because the comma after *terrain* inappropriately places a comma before *that*. D correctly places a comma only between the two adjectives. Note that you do not actually need to know anything about when to use a comma between *adjectives* to answer this question; it's really testing whether you know that commas don't belong between adjectives and nouns.

18. A: Add/delete/change

What is the sentence about? The way a person's voice is magnified. What is the previous sentence about? The fact that Schiphol is *a giant megaphone*. So logically, the sentence should be added because it provides more detail about the extent to which sound carries at the airport. That makes the answer A.

19. A: Diction

*Aggravate* means "make worse," which makes sense in context. A problem can be "aggravated," but it cannot be *exceeded* or *overloaded*. Careful with D: people can be irritated *by* a problem, but a problem itself cannot be irritated.

20. C: Transition

Start by crossing out the transition and determining the relationship between the two halves of the sentence. Part 1: The ridges deflected sound away from the ground. Part 2: Researchers decided to make the ridges (i.e. *that feature*) permanent. Logically, there is a cause-and-effect relationship. (Remember: researchers were trying to reduce noise, so they would want to make a

feature that deflected sound away from the ground permanent.) Only *because* conveys the correct relationship. A and B create illogical relationships, and D creates a comma splice.

21. B: Combining sentences, comma splice, passive voice

Since the sentences could be combined in any number of ways, you can work through the choices in order, making sure to plug them back into the sentence. A is grammatically acceptable, but it's also long and contains an awkward, passive construction (*a landscape is created by it that also serves…*) B: *The park, which officially opened in October 2013, makes use of meticulous yet simple landforms, creating a landscape that not only serves a specific function but is also an intriguing public space.* That's very long, but all of the options are long, and there's nothing inherently wrong with it. Furthermore, the verb *serves* agrees with its subject, *landscape*. If you're not sure, leave it. In C, the construction "comma + this" signals a comma splice. Eliminate it. Now plug in D, and read it carefully: *The park, which officially opened in October 2013, <u>makes</u> use of meticulous yet simple landforms and <u>creating</u> a landscape that not only serves a specific function but is also an intriguing public space.* The verb in the underlined portion must be parallel to *makes*, and here we don't have a conjugated verb (*creates*) but rather a gerund (*creating*). That eliminates D, leaving B.

22. C: Graphic

The graph represents the amount of noise in the Schiphol region in 2003 vs. 2013. The bar is about twice as high for 2003 than it is for 2013, indicating that airport noise decreased by about half (50%). A states that the airport noise was reduced "slightly," but 50% is much more than slightly. For B, don't even worry about the "more than half" part – the graph clearly indicates that noise levels in 2013 were *below* normal, not above. D is incorrect because 2013 levels were slightly below normal, not "significantly" below. That leaves C, which correctly states that noise levels were reduced by about half to "approximately" (i.e. slightly below) normal.

23. B: Colon, commas with list

Shortcut: if the words *including* or *such as* are used to set off a list, you do not need a colon after them. That eliminates A. Furthermore, a semicolon should not be used to set off a list because a list is not a full sentence. That eliminates C. The items in a list can be separated by either commas or semicolons, but only one or the other should be used. That eliminates D, leaving B.

24. D: Pronoun agreement

The underlined pronoun refers to the plural noun *digital archivists*. A plural pronoun (*they*) is therefore required.

25. B: Add/delete/change

What does the information that follows indicate? That photos from city or town parades get sent to newspapers in the area. What answer is most consistent with that idea? B, because the word *local* corresponds to *city or town parades*, and *in the area*. The other answers are generally consistent with the passage as a whole, but not with the information in the following sentence.

26. C: Pronouns

A is incorrect because the pronoun would logically refer to *newspapers*, making *there* the correct version of the pronoun. B does contain the word *place*, but it is too informal. D is incorrect because *this* is singular, and the pronoun would logically refer back to the plural noun *newspapers*. That leaves C, which uses a noun (*publications*) to specify where the photographs appear.

27. A: Add/delete/change

The question asks about the *process* of preserving images, so you're looking for information that specifically pertains to how images are preserved. If you don't recognize that A is consistent with that idea, check the remaining answers. B doesn't fit because *checking for problems once or twice a year* is something that would happen after the images were preserved; it wouldn't be part of the preservation process. C doesn't fit because the

focus must be on preserving the images, not on new technologies. D doesn't fit because again, the focus must be on the preservation process, not on archivists themselves. That leaves A.

28. D: Dashes

A non-essential clause that begins with a dash must end with a dash. That makes D the only option.

29. C: Pronoun agreement

Logically, the pronoun must refer to the plural noun *documents*. (What must be extracted with special tools? Documents.) As a result, a plural pronoun is required. That eliminates A and B. You would not say "… extract the documents from they are wrappings," so D can be eliminated as well. That leaves C, which correctly supplies the possessive *their*.

30. D: Sentence order

The phrase *blurry and unfocused* indicates that the sentence belongs in the part of the paragraph that discusses what happens when images aren't well preserved, so start by identifying the appropriate section. The necessary information appears in sentence 3 (*If images are not preserved properly…*). Logically, the sentence in question belongs after that sentence (i.e. before sentence 4) because it elaborates on the idea that sentence 3 expresses by describing another negative consequence of poor image preservation.

31. A: Sentence vs. fragment, transition

This is the rare instance in which the construction "comma + they" does not signal a comma splice. Here, the comma is correctly used to separate a fragment (*In addition to creating and maintaining databases that allow members of the public to locate specific records*) from a complete sentence (*they must advise users on how to access, use, and interpret archives*). Because a transition (*in addition*) appears at the beginning of the sentence, no transition should be used at the start of the second clause. Otherwise, an un-grammatical construction is created.

32. B: Parallel structure

The first two items in the list consist of conjugated verbs (*complete*, *pass*), so the third item must consist of a conjugated verb as well (*obtain*).

33. B: Non-essential vs. essential clause

Be very careful with this question. The two commas in the original version signal a non-essential clause, so try crossing the clause out of the sentence: *Individuals … must have at least a year of professional experience, while those with a degree in a different field must have at least two years of experience*. The sentence still makes grammatical sense, but an important piece of information has been lost: the word *while* indicates that there is a contrast between the first part of the sentence and *those with a degree in a different field*, but we no longer have the information necessary to make that contrast logical. The sentence only makes sense if the phrase *who have a graduate diploma in archival studies* is included. The phrase is therefore essential.

You can also think of it this way: the sentence is referring to a specific group of individuals – those who have a graduate diploma in archival studies. Using commas around the phrase would imply that the sentence was simply referring to individuals in general.

34. A: Graphic

Start by backing up and considering the entire sentence; you can't interpret the graph until you have the context for the underlined portion. The sentence compares the number of calculations per second made by a computer to the number made by an insect brain. In addition, it states that the number will be the same by 2020. Now look at the graph. The "insect brain" line is the bottom line, so that's all you need to worry about. Find 2020 on the x-axis. The line for "computing power" crosses the "insect brain" line right there, so the original version is correct.

35. D: Graphic

This sentence asks about 2060, so the easiest thing to do is jump to the graph and check 2060. The "computing power" line crosses the "one human brain" line there, indicating that computing power will equal that of a human brain in 2060. That makes the answer D.

36. A: Diction, idiom

The correct idiom is "not until x did y occur." In addition, *did* is the only option that can acceptably be paired with *begin*.

37. B: Comma, semicolon

The original version is incorrect because a semicolon should only be placed between two complete sentences; here, the information preceding the semicolon is a fragment. C is incorrect because a single comma should not normally come before a name. D is incorrect because a comma is necessary after *Eckert* to separate the introductory clause from the main clause. B correctly supplies the comma.

38. C: Add/delete/change

What does the information that follows the underlined phrase indicate? ENIAC was huge and heavy. The underlined information must therefore set up that idea. Only C fits – the description of the ENIAC's many parts corresponds to the idea that the computer was enormous.

39. C: Dangling modifier

Who finally realized that the tubes burned out less frequently if the computer was never turned off? Engineers. So *engineers*, the subject, must immediately follow the comma. That makes C the only possible answer.

40. A: Combining sentences

A correctly places a comma between a complete sentence (*Thousands of wires had to be plugged for each single instruction of a problem*) and the fragment that modifies it (*a process that could take weeks*). B is incorrect because the gerund *taking* creates a fragment. C is incorrect because *which could take weeks* is a fragment, and a semicolon should only be used to separate two sentences. D is incorrect because the construction "comma + this" creates a comma splice.

## 41. D: Register

A and C are both too informal, and B is too formal. D is consistent with the passage's straightforward, moderately serious tone.

## 42. C: Idiom, preposition

Known to be, known for = to have a reputation for; known as = called/named. Only the second option makes sense in context. D does not exist as an idiom.

## 43. A: Transition

Cross out the transition and consider the two halves of the sentence separately. Part 1: The EDVAC was large. Part 2: It was smaller and more powerful than the ENIAC. Those are opposing ideas, so a contradictor is required. *Consequently*, *as such*, and *likewise* are all continuers and can be eliminated. That leaves *nevertheless*, which is a contradictor (general synonym for *however*).

## 44. A: Add/delete/change

The key phrase in the question is *modern computers*, so the correct answer must have something to do with that idea. The option most consistent with that requirement is A, as indicated by the phrase *to this day*.

# Test 3 Answer Sheet

| | |
|---|---|
| 1. Ⓐ Ⓑ Ⓒ Ⓓ | 23. Ⓐ Ⓑ Ⓒ Ⓓ |
| 2. Ⓐ Ⓑ Ⓒ Ⓓ | 24. Ⓐ Ⓑ Ⓒ Ⓓ |
| 3. Ⓐ Ⓑ Ⓒ Ⓓ | 25. Ⓐ Ⓑ Ⓒ Ⓓ |
| 4. Ⓐ Ⓑ Ⓒ Ⓓ | 26. Ⓐ Ⓑ Ⓒ Ⓓ |
| 5. Ⓐ Ⓑ Ⓒ Ⓓ | 27. Ⓐ Ⓑ Ⓒ Ⓓ |
| 6. Ⓐ Ⓑ Ⓒ Ⓓ | 28. Ⓐ Ⓑ Ⓒ Ⓓ |
| 7. Ⓐ Ⓑ Ⓒ Ⓓ | 29. Ⓐ Ⓑ Ⓒ Ⓓ |
| 8. Ⓐ Ⓑ Ⓒ Ⓓ | 30. Ⓐ Ⓑ Ⓒ Ⓓ |
| 9. Ⓐ Ⓑ Ⓒ Ⓓ | 31. Ⓐ Ⓑ Ⓒ Ⓓ |
| 10. Ⓐ Ⓑ Ⓒ Ⓓ | 32. Ⓐ Ⓑ Ⓒ Ⓓ |
| 11. Ⓐ Ⓑ Ⓒ Ⓓ | 33. Ⓐ Ⓑ Ⓒ Ⓓ |
| 12. Ⓐ Ⓑ Ⓒ Ⓓ | 34. Ⓐ Ⓑ Ⓒ Ⓓ |
| 13. Ⓐ Ⓑ Ⓒ Ⓓ | 35. Ⓐ Ⓑ Ⓒ Ⓓ |
| 14. Ⓐ Ⓑ Ⓒ Ⓓ | 36. Ⓐ Ⓑ Ⓒ Ⓓ |
| 15. Ⓐ Ⓑ Ⓒ Ⓓ | 37. Ⓐ Ⓑ Ⓒ Ⓓ |
| 16. Ⓐ Ⓑ Ⓒ Ⓓ | 38. Ⓐ Ⓑ Ⓒ Ⓓ |
| 17. Ⓐ Ⓑ Ⓒ Ⓓ | 39. Ⓐ Ⓑ Ⓒ Ⓓ |
| 18. Ⓐ Ⓑ Ⓒ Ⓓ | 40. Ⓐ Ⓑ Ⓒ Ⓓ |
| 19. Ⓐ Ⓑ Ⓒ Ⓓ | 41. Ⓐ Ⓑ Ⓒ Ⓓ |
| 20. Ⓐ Ⓑ Ⓒ Ⓓ | 42. Ⓐ Ⓑ Ⓒ Ⓓ |
| 21. Ⓐ Ⓑ Ⓒ Ⓓ | 43. Ⓐ Ⓑ Ⓒ Ⓓ |
| 22. Ⓐ Ⓑ Ⓒ Ⓓ | 44. Ⓐ Ⓑ Ⓒ Ⓓ |

# Writing and Language Test
## 35 MINUTES, 44 QUESTIONS

**Turn to Section 2 of your answer sheet to answer the questions in this section.**

**Questions 1-11 are based on the following passage and supplemental information.**

**Life in the Bike Lane**

Every time a road is widened, a highway is constructed, or **1** people build a parking lot, the planet loses a bit more of its green space. While parks count a lot toward beauty and enjoyment of life, they also have more practical uses. **2** Therefore, they absorb carbon dioxide from the air and provide a habitat for wildlife.

**1**
A) NO CHANGE
B) they build a parking lot,
C) the building of parking lot occurs,
D) a parking lot is built,

**2**
A) NO CHANGE
B) For instance,
C) In contrast,
D) Nevertheless,

With each passing decade, however, the number of cars on the road in the United States has increased. In 2000, Americans owned **3** over 250 million more cars than they owned in 1960. People are also buying more cars than they once did. Moreover, while cars have consistently outnumbered drivers since the mid-twentieth century, that gap **4** began to increase after 2000. The result has been more roads, more garages, and more parking lots. The only way to slow the growth of automotive infrastructure is to reduce the number of cars, and replacing cars with bicycles could be part of the solution.

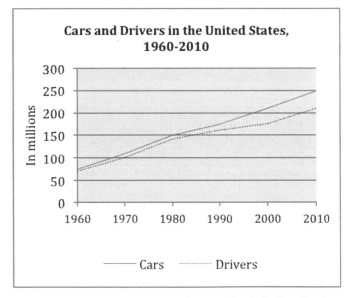

**Cars and Drivers in the United States, 1960-2010**

Source: Earth Policy Institute

Which choice offers an accurate interpretation of the information in the graph?

A) NO CHANGE

B) over 200 million more cars than they owned in 1960.

C) over 100 million more cars than they owned in 1960.

D) about the same number of cars that they owned in 1960.

Which choice offers an accurate interpretation of the information in the graph?

A) NO CHANGE

B) began to decrease after 2000.

C) began to increase during the 1980s.

D) began to decrease during the 1990s.

**5** The Automotive Industry in the United States began in the 1890s and rapidly evolved into the largest in the world. Several tons of waste and 1.2 billion cubic yards of polluted air are generated during manufacture alone. Each year, the painting and coating process produces almost 25 million pounds of hazardous waste. During **6** it's lifetime on the road, every car produces an additional 1.3 billion cubic yards of polluted air and **7** scattering an additional 40 pounds of tire particles, brake debris, and worn road surface into the atmosphere. If every car were replaced with a bicycle, virtually all that waste would disappear overnight.

A major advantage of bicycle infrastructure is that it costs significantly less to construct and maintain. **8** In fact, a road intended for cars can cost up to 2,500 times more than a pathway for bikes. The leftover funds would leave a lot more room for beautification projects, pollution clean-up, and other environmentally-oriented activities.

**5**

Which choice provides the most appropriate introduction to the paragraph?

A) NO CHANGE
B) From the foam and plastic in its seats to the petroleum in its tires, each car is a small pollution factory.
C) By the end of the 1920s, the automotive industry was dominated by three large companies: General Motors, Ford, and Chrysler.
D) During the post-World War II period, cars grew larger and began to feature more amenities.

**6**

A) NO CHANGE
B) its
C) they're
D) their

**7**

A) NO CHANGE
B) scatters
C) scatter
D) scattered

**8**

A) NO CHANGE
B) In contrast,
C) Despite this,
D) Consequently,

Businesses can encourage the use of bicycles by improving bicycle access to buildings and facilities. They can, for example, install racks where employees and customers can **9** securely store their bicycles in a safe place. In addition, they can distribute information about bike routes and bicycle-friendly public transportation connections. Finally, **10** they can create social opportunities for bikers such as arranging for employee discounts at local bike shops or bonuses for employees who bike to work.

In the 1980s, the biologist Edward O. Wilson hypothesized that human beings were innately drawn to the natural world, and that our connection to nature is essential to our wellbeing. Flying down a garden path instead of **11** lumbering down a highway not only helps give the planet a makeover but it also provides an important opportunity to relax and recharge.

**9**

A) NO CHANGE
B) securely store their bicycles in a way that is safe.
C) securely store their bicycles.
D) securely store their bicycles in safety.

**10**

Which choice most effectively sets up the examples that follow?

A) NO CHANGE
B) they can provide opportunities for employees to get in shape
C) hand out flyers describing the health benefits of biking
D) they can offer financial incentives

**11**

A) NO CHANGE
B) stammering
C) wafting
D) exploring

**Questions 12-22 are based on the following passage.**

## Hot Potato

Every time a person crunches into a potato chip, **12** you are enjoying the delicious taste of one of the world's most famous snacks. It a treat that might not have existed without the contribution of inventor George Crum. Born to an African American father and a Native American mother in 1828, Crumb was raised in **13** upstate New York, he trained as a chef there as well.

In the summer of 1853, Crum was employed at Moon Lake Lodge an elegant hotel in the resort town of Saratoga Springs. Among the items on Moon Lake Lodge's restaurant menu were French-fried potatoes. Every day, Crum prepared them in the standard thick-cut style that had been popularized in France, **14** whose capital is Paris, and brought back to the United States by Thomas Jefferson after he finished serving as the American ambassador.

**12**
A) NO CHANGE
B) one is
C) they are
D) he or she is

**13**
A) NO CHANGE
B) upstate New York; training as a chef there as well.
C) upstate New York, it was there that he trained as a chef also.
D) upstate New York, where he also trained as a chef.

**14**
The writer is considering deleting the underlined portion (adjusting the punctuation accordingly). Should it be kept or deleted?

A) Kept, because it specifies where thick-cut potatoes originated.
B) Kept, because it describes a foreign influence on cooking in the United States.
C) Deleted, because it blurs the paragraph's focus on the menu at Moon Lodge.
D) Deleted, because Crum only worked in upstate New York.

Crum's thick-cut potatoes were popular at Moon Lake Lodge, **15** and many prominent individuals consumed them each summer. Crum cut and fried a thinner batch, but they also met with disapproval. Exasperated, Crum decided to teach the guest a **16** lesson, but he produced potato slices that were too thin and crisp to skewer with a fork. He sliced a new batch of potatoes as thin as he possibly could. **17** Therefore, he fried them until they were hard and crunchy. To top them off, he added a generous heaping of salt.

Crumb was prepared for the guest to be disappointed yet again, but instead he was ecstatic about the browned, paper-thin potatoes. The guest's excitement was contagious, and other diners quickly asked to try them. **18** A new snack was born.

**15**

Which choice most effectively sets up the information that follows?

A) NO CHANGE

B) but one evening an unsatisfied guest requested that Crum bring him thinner slices.

C) and patrons often chose to eat there rather than at other local establishments.

D) but other restaurants in the region served them as well.

**16**

A) NO CHANGE

B) lesson and producing

C) lesson: he produced

D) lesson; producing

**17**

A) NO CHANGE

B) Then,

C) Consequently,

D) However,

**18**

The writer is considering adding the following sentence.

> Crum's potatoes were soon in such high demand that they were added to the menu as "Saratoga chips."

Should the writer make this addition?

A) Yes, because it adds relevant detail illustrating the popularity of Crum's invention.

B) Yes, because it supports the idea that Crum enjoyed defying convention.

C) No, because it distracts from the paragraph's focus on the diners at Moon Lake Lodge.

D) No, because it interrupts the logical development of the paragraph.

Seven years later, Crum opened his own restaurant, which **19** conveyed a basket of potato chips on every table. Within a few years he was catering to wealthy clients, including the Vanderbilts, Jay Gould, and Henry Hilton. By the time the restaurant closed in 1892, potato chips **20** have become a staple of Northern cooking. Though Crum never attempted to patent his invention, the snack was eventually mass-produced and **21** they sold it in bags. In the 1920s, the invention of the mechanical potato peeler paved the way for potato chips to shift from a specialty item to a top-selling snack food.

Today, potatoes are second in human consumption only to rice. And as **22** thin, salted, crispy chips, they are the top-selling snack food in the United States.

**19**
A) NO CHANGE
B) featured
C) revealed
D) elaborated

**20**
A) NO CHANGE
B) will become
C) had become
D) becoming

**21**
A) NO CHANGE
B) sold
C) selling
D) being sold

**22**
A) NO CHANGE
B) thin, salted, crispy chips –
C) thin; salted, crispy, chips,
D) thin, salted, crispy chips;

**Questions 23-33 are based on the following passage.**

**Rings of Saturn**

　　Beautiful, glamorous and mysterious, Saturn's rings are among the most recognizable features in the solar system. While the solar system's other three gas giants – Jupiter, Uranus and Neptune – have rings orbiting around **23** them; Saturn is by far the largest and most spectacular. They spread over hundreds of thousands of miles, yet they are only around 30 feet thick. They consist of billions of individual particles, which create **24** waves, turbulence, and other affects.

　　The rings are believed to be pieces of comets, asteroids, or shattered moons that broke up before they reached the planet, and each of them **25** orbit at a different speed. They are made up of billions of particles that range in size from tiny, dust-like icy grains to **26** rocky meteoroids. Two tiny moons orbit in gaps in the rings, keeping the gaps open. Other particles are too tiny to see but create propeller-shaped objects within the rings.

**23**

A) NO CHANGE
B) them, Saturn
C) them. Saturn
D) them, and Saturn

**24**

A) NO CHANGE
B) waves, turbulence; and other affects.
C) waves, turbulence, and, other effects.
D) waves, turbulence, and other effects.

**25**

A) NO CHANGE
B) orbits
C) have orbited
D) orbiting

**26**

Which choice most logically completes the sentence?

A) NO CHANGE
B) small mineral fragments.
C) mountain-sized objects.
D) frozen materials.

[1] The rings have been **27** a mysterious object since the astronomer, Galileo Galilei discovered them with his telescope in 1610. [2] In the 1980s, the spacecrafts Voyager 1 and Voyager 2 were sent to study the rings, but their mystery only increased. [3] More importantly, it might explain why they're there in the first place. [4] In July of 2004, researchers at NASA's Jet Propulsion Laboratory in Pasadena, California launched a spacecraft consisting of the Cassini orbiter and the Huygens probe. [5] Information from the Cassini mission could help reveal how the rings formed and how they maintain their orbit. **28**

**27**

A) NO CHANGE
B) a mysterious object since the astronomer
C) mysterious objects since the astronomer,
D) mysterious objects since the astronomer

**28**

What is the best place for sentence 3?

A) where it is now.
B) After sentence 1.
C) After sentence 4.
D) After sentence 5.

In some ways, the Cassini spacecraft has senses [29] better than a person. The instruments on the spacecraft can "feel" things about magnetic fields and tiny dust particles that no human hand could possibly detect.

[30] Indeed, the spacecraft began returning valuable information about the rings even before it slipped into Saturn's orbit. During the orbital insertion maneuver, the spacecraft obtained data about ring structure, including stunning high-resolution images.

Furthermore, [31] Cassini is one of the largest, heaviest and most complex interplanetary spacecraft ever built. For instance, the probe found that the expansive E ring is composed primarily of icy material from the moon Enceladus, while Saturn's inner moons appear to orbit within rings formed from particles blasted off [32] their surfaces by micrometeoroid impacts.

[29]

A) NO CHANGE
B) better than a person can sense things.
C) better than a person's senses.
D) better than what a person has.

[30]

A) NO CHANGE
B) However,
C) Otherwise,
D) For example,

[31]

Which choice most logically sets up the examples that follow?

A) NO CHANGE
B) data from Cassini indicated that the rings we observe today have different origins.
C) Cassini's instruments are often programmed to have a variety of functions.
D) The spacecraft communicates with Earth through its antenna subsystem.

[32]

A) NO CHANGE
B) they're surfaces
C) its surfaces
D) these surface's

One question that researchers have not yet answered is how old Saturn's rings are. Some scientists believe that they date back to the early history of the Solar System, while other claim that they formed as recently as the age of dinosaurs. [33] Cassini will look for signs of seasonal climate change such as storms, flooding, or changes in lake levels, as well as evidence of volcanic activity.

Which choice most logically concludes the passage while reinforcing its main theme?

A) NO CHANGE

B) Cassini completed its initial four-year mission to explore the Saturn System in June 2008 and began a second mission in 2010.

C) Cassini scientists are hopeful that their work will reveal new insights into this enduring mystery.

D) Cassini discovered an icy plume shooting from the moon Enceladus, and subsequent observations have revealed the spray contains complex organic chemicals.

**Questions 34-44 are based on the following passage.**

**The Practical Writer**

If you've ever put together a piece of furniture, set up a new appliance, or installed a new program on your computer, you probably followed a set of directions written by a technical writer. Technical writing is sometimes defined as "simplifying the complex." Although many people today associate this career exclusively with computers and **34** software, but the practice of technical writing can take place in any field or industry that involves complex ideas or procedures. **35** Good technical writing provides relevant, useful and accurate information, which may be presented in the form of user guides, operating and instruction manuals, or graphics.

**34**

A) NO CHANGE
B) software; but
C) software –
D) software,

**35**

At this point, the writer is considering adding the following sentence.

> Technical writers can provide instruction on everything from preparing a meal to repairing an engine.

Should the writer make this addition?

A) Yes, because it describes how technical writers locate relevant information.
B) Yes, because it provides specific examples of fields that involve technical writing.
C) No, because it does not refer to fields that involve complex procedures.
D) No, because it does not explain how technical writers go about simplifying complex information.

Technical writing has been around as long as there have been written languages. **36** Likewise, modern references to technical writing as a profession first appeared around the time of World War I. At that time, developments in industry and telecommunications began to evolve more rapidly. In the 1960s, demand for technical writers **37** upheld as a result of the continued growth of technology, particularly in the electronics, aeronautics, and space industries. The field got an additional boost in 1975, when the United States Government passed a law requiring that all manufacturers clearly state their warranties. Today, the Internet offers countless opportunities for technical **38** writers. Many of whom will design and develop future generations of online help systems.

**36**

A) NO CHANGE
B) Moreover,
C) In fact,
D) However,

**37**

A) NO CHANGE
B) flew
C) elevated
D) soared

**38**

A) NO CHANGE
B) writers, many of which
C) writers, many of whom
D) writers, many of them

**39** Technical writers must be able to distill complex information into clear, concise text, they must have excellent written communication and grammar skills and be able to work independently in order to deliver accurate documentation under deadline pressure. Many technical writers therefore hold degrees in English or other subjects that require large amounts of writing. At the same time, **40** he or she must also be familiar with a variety of specialized software programs in order to create charts or **41** insert diagrams. Some technical writing jobs also require editing, proofreading, and document publishing abilities. As people **42** chitchat way more through online media, skills such as blogging, Web design, and video production are becoming increasingly important.

**39**

A) NO CHANGE
B) Because technical writers
C) Whereas technical writers
D) Although technical writers

**40**

A) NO CHANGE
B) one
C) you
D) they

**41**

Which choice gives a second supporting example that is most similar to the example already in the sentence?

A) NO CHANGE
B) describe detailed processes.
C) provide instructions.
D) engage readers.

**42**

Which choice best maintains the tone established in the passage?

A) NO CHANGE
B) increasingly communicate
C) express what they think a lot of the time
D) convey their musings in greater quantities

While technical writers might once have primarily worked independently **43** for the most part, today their jobs require them to collaborate with many different workers. This is particularly true during development and testing periods, when they must manage the flow of information among project workgroups. As a result, technical writers must not only understand complex information **44** but also being able to communicate it to people with diverse professional backgrounds.

**43**

A) NO CHANGE
B) on the whole,
C) generally speaking,
D) DELETE the underlined phrase.

**44**

A) NO CHANGE
B) but also be able
C) with being able
D) and also be able

**Test 3: Explanations**

1. D: Parallel structure

Consider the construction of the other two items in the list: noun + is + -ed. The underlined item must appear in the same format. Only D contains the correct construction.

2. B: Transition

Cross out the transition and consider the relationship between the sentence in question and the previous sentence. Sentence 1: Parks have practical uses. Sentence 2: They absorb carbon and house wildlife. Logically, the second sentence is giving examples of practical uses. *For instance* is the only transition that correctly expresses that relationship.

3. C: Graphic

Start by reading the entire sentence in which the underlined portion appears. It provides two key pieces of information: you're dealing with 1) the number of cars (solid line) and 2) the difference between 1960 and 2000. Since the line goes up very markedly, you can immediately eliminate D. Now, look at the numbers. The line for 1960 crosses at about 75 million, whereas the line for 2000 crosses at 200 million. That's a difference of about 125 million, or "over 100 million," making the answer C.

4. C: Graphic

Make sure you're clear on what the graph is showing before you start trying to answer the question; otherwise, you could get distracted by the fact that one of the lines dips lower than the other. The solid line represents the number of cars, whereas the dotted line represents the number of drivers. Both increased between 1960 and 1990, but the number of cars increased more. In other words, the gap between the number of cars and the number of drivers *increased*. That eliminates B and D. When did the lines begin to diverge? Sometime between 1980 and 1990, making the answer C. Although the gap was at its largest between 2000 and 2010, it remained stable during that period.

5. B: Add/delete/change

What is the focus of the paragraph? The fact that cars produce a huge amount of pollution. The correct answer must therefore introduce that idea. The phrase *each car is a small pollution factory* in B directly corresponds to it.

6. B: Pronoun agreement, apostrophes

The underlined pronoun refers to the noun *every car*, which is singular. (Note that while nouns typically come before the pronouns that refer to them, in this case the pronoun comes first.) A singular pronoun is required, eliminating C and D. Since you would not say "During it is lifetime," the possessive *its* is correct.

7. B: Parallel structure

The underlined verb must be parallel in tense and form to the other verb in the sentence, *produces*. It must also agree with the singular subject *each car*. Only *scatters* fulfills those criteria.

8. A: Transition

Cross out the transition and determine the relationship between the sentence in question and the previous sentence. Sentence 1: Bicycle infrastructure costs less than car infrastructure. Sentence 2: A road for cars can cost $2,500 more than a road for bicycles. Those are similar ideas, so B and C can be eliminated. The second sentence is also not a result of the first, so D can be eliminated as well. That leaves the original version, which correctly indicates that the second sentence expands upon the first.

9. C: Redundancy, shorter is better

*Securely* means "safely," so it is redundant to include both words.

10. D: Add/delete/change

What is the focus of the examples at the end of the sentence? Discounts and bonuses. The correct answer must therefore have something to do with money. The phrase *financial incentives* in D is most consistent with this idea.

## 11. A: Diction

The word *instead* indicates that the underlined word means the opposite of *flying*. *Stammering* means "stuttering" – it's used to refer to speech, not movement. *Wafting* means "drifting" – it's normally used for smells. *Exploring* simply doesn't make sense. That leaves A. *Lumbering* evokes the clumsy movement of something very large, which fits as the opposite of flying.

## 12. D: Pronoun agreement

The underlined pronoun must agree with the singular noun *a person*, making the singular *he or she* the only option.

## 13. D: Comma splice

The constructions "comma + he" in the original version and "comma + it" in C signal comma splices. B is incorrect because a semicolon should only be used to separate two complete sentences, and the phrase after the semicolon is a fragment. D is correct because it places a comma between a complete sentence and a fragment, and because it appropriately uses *where* to refer to a place.

## 14. C: Add/delete/change

What is the focus of the underlined portion? Geographical information about France. What is the focus of the paragraph? Why thick-cut potatoes were popular in the 1850s. Is the underlined portion relevant? No, it's off-topic. So the answer is C.

## 15. B: Add/delete/change

What is the focus of the information after the underlined portion? The fact that someone wasn't happy with Crum's potatoes. Only the phrase *a dissatisfied guest* in B is consistent with that idea.

## 16. C: Transition, colon

Since the underlined portion includes a transition, start by determining the relationship between the two halves of the sentence. Part 1: Crum wanted to teach a lesson to the guest who complained his potatoes weren't thin enough. Part 2: He cut the potatoes too thin to eat with a fork. Logically, the second half is the result of the first, so the contradictor *but* creates an illogical relationship. B doesn't work since the gerund *producing* creates a fragment. D is incorrect because a semicolon should only be used to separate two complete sentences, and the phrase after the semicolon is a fragment, as signaled by the gerund *producing*. That leaves C, which uses a colon to signal that the second part of the sentence expands on the first (it explains *how* Crum decided to teach the guest a lesson).

## 17. B: Transition

Start by crossing out the transition and determining the relationship between the sentence in question and the previous sentence. Sentence 1: Crum sliced more potatoes as thin as he could. Sentence 2: Crum fried the potatoes until they were hard and crunchy. Those are steps in a sequence; the second part isn't the result of the first, as *therefore* would indicate. Only *then* makes sense in context.

## 18. A: Add/delete/change

What is the sentence to be added about? The fact that Crum's potatoes quickly became very popular. What is the paragraph about? The excitement over Crum's potatoes. Does the sentence fit? Yes. Since the passage does not indicate that Crum enjoyed defying convention beyond the single incident of the potatoes, the answer is A.

## 19. B: Diction

Given the context, the underlined word must mean something like "displayed." The word closest in meaning is *featured*.

## 20. C: Tense

The date 1892 indicates that the past tense must be used. In the original version, *have become* (present perfect) is incorrect because this tense refers to an action that is continuing into the present. *Will become* is future, so B can be eliminated. D is incorrect because the gerund *becoming* creates a fragment. C is the only option that contains a verb in the past tense. **Shortcut:** the phrase *by the time* is a tip-off that the past perfect (had + verb) is required.

21. B: Parallel structure, pronoun agreement

In the original version, the pronoun *they* is missing a referent – the sentence does not specify who *they* are. B is correct because the verb *was* "applies" to both *mass produced* and *sold*; there is no need to repeat the verb before *sold*. C is incorrect because the gerund *selling* creates a nonsense meaning: the snack *was sold* – it wasn't *selling* anything. D is incorrect because the gerund *being* creates an awkward construction that is not parallel to *mass-produced*.

22. A: Commas with list

The original version correctly separates the items in the list with commas and places an additional comma after *chips* to separate the first clause (fragment) from the second clause (sentence). B is incorrect because a single dash should come after a complete sentence. C is incorrect because either commas or semicolons should separate items in a list; the two should not be mixed and matched. D is incorrect because a semicolon should only separate two complete sentences, and the phrase before the semicolon is a fragment.

23. B: Semicolon, comma

A period, a semicolon, and "comma + and" are all grammatically identical and can therefore be eliminated. That leaves B, which correctly places a comma between a fragment (*While the solar system's other three gas giants – Jupiter, Uranus and Neptune – have rings orbiting around them*) and a sentence (*Saturn is by far the largest and most spectacular*).

24. D: Diction, commas with list

*Affect* is a verb, whereas *effect* is a noun. (There are exceptions, but you don't need to worry about them here.) A noun is required in this context, eliminating A and B. C is incorrect because no comma is required after the word *and*, and before the last item in a list.

25. B: Subject-verb agreement

*Each* is singular and requires a singular verb (*orbits*). The tense change in C is a distraction; *have* is plural, so this answer cannot be right. D is incorrect because the gerund *orbiting* creates a fragment. B is the only possible answer.

26. C: Add/delete/change

The construction *from tiny, dust-like icy grains to*… indicates that the underlined phrase must refer to something that is the opposite of tiny. *Mountain-sized objects* would clearly be very large, so C is correct. *Rocky meteoroids* and *frozen materials* are not necessarily large or small, and *small mineral fragments* are clearly not the opposite of something tiny.

27. D: Noun agreement, comma with name

*Rings* is plural, so they are "mysterious objects" rather than "a mysterious object." That eliminates A and B. C is incorrect because when a name appears in the middle of a sentence, it should not only be preceded by a comma. (Commas before and after are acceptable, as is a comma after).

28. D: Sentence order

Sentence 2 indicates that the Voyager missions failed to reveal anything about Saturn's rings, so the statement that *it might explain why they're there in the first place* doesn't logically follow. That eliminates A. Sentence 1 talks about Galileo and the seventeenth century, which is completely unrelated to sentence 3. Eliminate B. Sentence 3 doesn't fit after sentence 4 either; the phrase *More importantly* indicates that the end of the previous sentence must refer to something less important that could be explained. That eliminates C. The only remaining option is D, which is correct because sentence 5 does refer to another mystery that Cassini could help explain.

29. C: Faulty comparison

The original version compares senses (things) to a person. To correct the sentence, senses must be compared to senses. The comparison is correctly formed in C.

## 30. A: Transition

Start by crossing out the original transition and considering the relationship between the sentence in question and the previous question. Sentence 1: Cassini's instruments are extraordinarily sensitive. Sentence 2: Cassini began returning valuable information right away. Those are similar ideas, so B and C can both be eliminated. D doesn't fit since the second sentence isn't actually an example of the first; it simply builds on it. That leaves A, which conveys the correct relationship.

## 31. B: Add/delete/change

What is the focus of the examples that follow? Different rings are made of different materials. That has nothing to do with Cassini's size, instruments, or communication system, so A, C, and D can be eliminated. The idea that the rings have different origins is consistent with the idea that their composition varies, so B is correct.

## 32. A: Pronoun agreement, apostrophes

The underlined pronoun refers to the plural noun *particles*, so the pronoun must be plural as well. *It* is singular, so C can be eliminated. You would not say "… particles blasted off they are surfaces," so *their* is the correct form. That eliminates B. D is incorrect because *surfaces* is plural, not possessive, and plural nouns do not take apostrophes. That leaves A, which uses the correct form of the possessive pronoun *their* and the plural noun *surfaces*.

## 33. C: Add/delete/change

If you haven't been paying attention to what the passage is about, you don't have to go back and read the whole thing. Logically, the final sentence must connect to the final paragraph, so you can start by rereading the final paragraph. What does it discuss? That the age of Saturn's rings is unknown. The phrase *this enduring mystery* in C corresponds to that idea. If you want to check it out, you can reread the first sentence of the passage, which also indicates that Saturn's rings are "mysterious."

## 34. D: Transition, semicolon, comma

Because *although* appears at the beginning of the sentence, *but* should not be used as well. That eliminates A. B is incorrect because a semicolon should not be used before *but*. C is incorrect because a complete sentence should precede a single dash, and the phrase before the dash is a fragment. D correctly places a comma between a fragment (*Although many people today associate this career exclusively with computers and software*) and a sentence (*the practice of technical writing can take place in any field or industry that involves complex ideas or procedures*).

## 35. B: Add/delete/change

What is the focus of the sentence? Different areas in which technical writers can provide instruction. What is the focus of the paragraph? The fact that technical writing is found in lots of different areas. Are those ideas similar or different? Similar. So the sentence should be added. A can be eliminated because the sentence says nothing specific about how technical writers locate relevant information; it only provides examples of specific areas in which technical writing can be found. The answer is therefore B.

## 36. D: Transition

Start by crossing out the original transition and considering the relationship between the sentence in question and the previous question. Sentence 1: Technical writing has been around for a really long time (thousands of years). Sentence 2: Technical writing didn't become a profession until World War I (pretty recently). Those are contrasting ideas, so D is the only possibility.

## 37. D: Diction

The phrase *continued growth* indicates that the underlined word must be a synonym for "increased." Only *soared* can be used idiomatically to have this meaning.

38.  C: Sentence vs. fragment

A sentence cannot begin with *many of whom*; this construction signals a fragment, which must follow a comma rather than a period. That eliminates A and makes C correct. B is incorrect because *which* refers to things, not people. D is incorrect because *many of them* can begin a sentence; as a result, the comma before that phrase creates a comma splice.

39.  B: Transition, comma splice

Make sure you read all the way to the end of the sentence. Although the beginning of the original version works just fine, that answer actually creates a comma splice. Note the construction "comma + they" later in the sentence. In order to eliminate the comma splice, the first clause must be made dependent. A transition is therefore necessary. C and D are both contradictors and can be eliminated; that leaves B, which correctly indicates the cause-and-effect relationship between the clauses.

40.  D: Pronoun agreement

The underlined pronoun must refer to the plural noun *technical writers*. A plural pronoun (*they*) is therefore required.

41.  A: Add/delete/change

The example already in the sentence involves charts, and diagrams are most similar to charts. They are also the only option that could only be created by *specialized software programs*.

42.  B: Register, shorter is better

A and C are both far too casual, whereas D is excessively formal. In addition, C and D are both unnecessarily wordy.

43.  D: Redundancy, shorter is better

*Primarily*, *on the whole*, *generally speaking*, and *for the most part* all have the same meaning. Only one of those words/phrases should be used.

44.  B: Word pair, parallel structure

*Not only* must be paired with *but also*. That eliminates C and D. The construction must also be the same on either side of the word pair: *not only* is followed by a verb (*understand*), so *but also* must be followed by a verb as well (*be*). That makes B correct.

# Test 4 Answer Sheet

1. Ⓐ Ⓑ Ⓒ Ⓓ
2. Ⓐ Ⓑ Ⓒ Ⓓ
3. Ⓐ Ⓑ Ⓒ Ⓓ
4. Ⓐ Ⓑ Ⓒ Ⓓ
5. Ⓐ Ⓑ Ⓒ Ⓓ
6. Ⓐ Ⓑ Ⓒ Ⓓ
7. Ⓐ Ⓑ Ⓒ Ⓓ
8. Ⓐ Ⓑ Ⓒ Ⓓ
9. Ⓐ Ⓑ Ⓒ Ⓓ
10. Ⓐ Ⓑ Ⓒ Ⓓ
11. Ⓐ Ⓑ Ⓒ Ⓓ
12. Ⓐ Ⓑ Ⓒ Ⓓ
13. Ⓐ Ⓑ Ⓒ Ⓓ
14. Ⓐ Ⓑ Ⓒ Ⓓ
15. Ⓐ Ⓑ Ⓒ Ⓓ
16. Ⓐ Ⓑ Ⓒ Ⓓ
17. Ⓐ Ⓑ Ⓒ Ⓓ
18. Ⓐ Ⓑ Ⓒ Ⓓ
19. Ⓐ Ⓑ Ⓒ Ⓓ
20. Ⓐ Ⓑ Ⓒ Ⓓ
21. Ⓐ Ⓑ Ⓒ Ⓓ
22. Ⓐ Ⓑ Ⓒ Ⓓ

23. Ⓐ Ⓑ Ⓒ Ⓓ
24. Ⓐ Ⓑ Ⓒ Ⓓ
25. Ⓐ Ⓑ Ⓒ Ⓓ
26. Ⓐ Ⓑ Ⓒ Ⓓ
27. Ⓐ Ⓑ Ⓒ Ⓓ
28. Ⓐ Ⓑ Ⓒ Ⓓ
29. Ⓐ Ⓑ Ⓒ Ⓓ
30. Ⓐ Ⓑ Ⓒ Ⓓ
31. Ⓐ Ⓑ Ⓒ Ⓓ
32. Ⓐ Ⓑ Ⓒ Ⓓ
33. Ⓐ Ⓑ Ⓒ Ⓓ
34. Ⓐ Ⓑ Ⓒ Ⓓ
35. Ⓐ Ⓑ Ⓒ Ⓓ
36. Ⓐ Ⓑ Ⓒ Ⓓ
37. Ⓐ Ⓑ Ⓒ Ⓓ
38. Ⓐ Ⓑ Ⓒ Ⓓ
39. Ⓐ Ⓑ Ⓒ Ⓓ
40. Ⓐ Ⓑ Ⓒ Ⓓ
41. Ⓐ Ⓑ Ⓒ Ⓓ
42. Ⓐ Ⓑ Ⓒ Ⓓ
43. Ⓐ Ⓑ Ⓒ Ⓓ
44. Ⓐ Ⓑ Ⓒ Ⓓ

# Writing and Language Test
## 35 MINUTES, 44 QUESTIONS

**Turn to Section 2 of your answer sheet to answer the questions in this section.**

**Questions 1-11 are based on the following passage.**

A Capital Tale

– 1 –

Benjamin Banneker was an inventor. He was also an astronomer, writer, and **1** working as a city planner. One of the few African Americans to earn international distinction in science during the nineteenth century, he built a wooden clock from scratch, published a famous almanac, and campaigned against slavery. And were it not for him, the city of Washington, D.C. as it appears today would not exist.

**1**

A) NO CHANGE
B) being a city planner.
C) city planner.
D) to work as a city planner.

– 2 –

Shortly after the end of the Revolutionary War, George Washington hired the French **2** <u>architect, Pierre L'Enfant</u> to design the plans for the new capital. L'Enfant was young – only 22 years old – and enthusiastic about designing a capital city that would remain a district apart from the states themselves. He **3** <u>exhibited</u> a grand metropolis that would include nearly 10 square miles and be full of broad, sweeping boulevards.

– 3 –

Unfortunately, designing the capital proved to be easier than building it. **4** Stubborn and short-tempered, **5** <u>clashes between L'Enfant and the other members of the planning committee quickly occurred.</u> In 1792, only a year after he had begun work on the project, L'Enfant was fired. He stormed away, taking all of the plans for the city with him.

**2**

A) NO CHANGE
B) architect, Pierre L'Enfant,
C) architect Pierre L'Enfant
D) architect: Pierre L'Enfant

**3**

A) NO CHANGE
B) envisioned
C) imported
D) predicted

**4**

At this point, the writer wants to add specific information that supports the main topic of the paragraph.

A) The project experienced numerous delays, and construction proceeded more slowly than anyone had expected.
B) Both Thomas Jefferson and George Washington agreed that Washington, DC should be located on a main waterway.
C) L'Enfant's plan for a tract encompassing 10 square miles rejected Jefferson's preference for a small village that would gradually expand.
D) L'Enfant was so inspired by the cause of America's Revolutionary War that he had volunteered to serve in the conflict.

**5**

A) NO CHANGE
B) L'Enfant quickly clashed with the other members of the planning committee.
C) the result of L'Enfant's behavior was clashes between him and the other members of the planning committee.
D) the occurrence of clashes between L'Enfant and the other members of the planning committee was quick.

– 4 –

When L'Enfant disappeared along with his plans, Banneker stepped in and, as legend has it, salvaged the entire project. As the story goes, he reproduced L'Enfant's entire plan, including every last street, park, and important building. What's more, he **6** accomplished this feat in only two days. Thus, the city of Washington, D.C. can be considered a testament to Banneker's extraordinary talent.

– 5 –

Enter Benjamin Banneker. In the early 1790s, Banneker was known as expert in a variety of fields. He had accurately predicted the dates of solar eclipses and designed a farm whose crops kept American troops from starving during the Revolutionary War. Furthermore, Banneker was beginning to establish an international reputation. **7** In 1788, Banneker began a more formal study of astrology. Impressed by Banneker's numerous **8** accomplishments, Thomas Jefferson, who recommended that Banneker be appointed to the surveying team responsible for **9** lying out the city of Washington, D.C.

**6**
A) NO CHANGE
B) did this thing
C) consummated this endeavor
D) finished this idea

**7**
Which choice best supports the statement made in the previous sentence?

A) NO CHANGE
B) As a teenager, Banneker befriended Peter Heinrichs, a Quaker who established a school near the Banneker farm.
C) His almanacs were read in countries as far away as England and France.
D) Banneker expressed his views on equality in a series of letters to Thomas Jefferson.

**8**
A) NO CHANGE
B) accomplishments; Thomas Jefferson
C) accomplishments, and Thomas Jefferson
D) accomplishments, Thomas Jefferson

**9**
A) NO CHANGE
B) laying out
C) stretching out
D) elongating

– 6 –

Today, some historians question whether Banneker's role in reconstructing L'Enfant's plan was exaggerated. **10** However, it seems improbable that he was singlehandedly capable of recalling every last detail. More likely, the other members of the surveying committee played a significant part as well. What is not up for dispute, however, is Banneker's legacy. He used his reputation to promote social change and to eliminate racism and war. In his later years, he won friends and admirers both in the United States and abroad, serving as an inspiration to people around the world. **11**

**10**

A) NO CHANGE
B) Indeed,
C) Meanwhile,
D) Consequently,

**Think about the passage as a whole as you answer question 11.**

**11**

To make the passage most logical, paragraph 5 should be placed

A) where it is now.
B) after paragraph 1.
C) after paragraph 2.
D) after paragraph 3.

**Questions 12-22 are based on the following passage.**

**The Dancing Lion**

Ornately decorated lion heads with bright, wide eyes bob and dodge their way among the crowds. From beneath my mask, I can see the crowds laughing and cheering. I am a Chinese Lion dancer. As a child, I always loved watching the lion dancers, and my siblings and I would even try to imitate **12** they're movements. When I got a little older, I studied the martial arts that strongly influenced Lion Dancing; however, it was not until I began college that I joined my first Lion Dancing troupe.

Since the Han Dynasty (180-230 A.D.), Lion Dancing **13** is an important Chinese tradition – one that has now been transported around the world. **14** It was first performed as a demonstration of martial arts skills. It later evolved to take the lion's expression and natural movements into account. Today, my fellow dancers and I take to the stage for celebrations including anniversaries, birthdays, and store openings. We also dance in parades for festivals such as Chinese New Year.

**12**

A) NO CHANGE
B) their
C) there
D) his or her

**13**

A) NO CHANGE
B) was
C) has been
D) would be

**14**

Which choice most effectively combines the sentences at the underlined portion?

A) First being performed as a demonstration of martial arts skills and later evolving to take the lion's expression and natural movements into account.

B) First performed as a demonstration of martial arts skills, it later evolved to take the lion's expression and natural movements into account.

C) First performed as a demonstration of martial arts skills, the lion's expression and natural movements were later taken into account.

D) It was first performed as a demonstration of martial arts skills, but the evolution to take the lion's expression and natural movements into account came later.

For dances in the northern style, the other dancers and I wear lion costumes with shaggy yellow fur and long manes. **15** Our pants are yellow, similar to the fur, and our shoes are decorated to resemble lions' claws. As a result, our movements are lifelike, and we often use our legs to prance dramatically. We also dance in family pairs: two adult lions and two young lions. These dances require great agility. We perform stunts such as balancing on balls, lifting one another up, and **16** banging on drums.

Southern Chinese Lion Dancing is based on an ancient **17** tale that originated a very long time ago. Terrorized by a mythical monster, a group of villagers huddled under an enormous monster of their own in an attempt to repel the beast. As a result, the southern "lion" resembles a dragon. It thrusts its head to the **18** sound of: drums, gongs and cymbals, and we must precisely coordinate our movements with the rhythm of the instruments. Our costumes are red, symbolizing bravery; green, symbolizing friendship and goodwill; and **19** a lively, dynamic spirit is symbolized by gold. At each performance, we repeat the ritual to the accompaniment of firecracker bursts and drums.

---

**15**

Which choice most effectively sets up the sentence that follows?

A) NO CHANGE

B) The Chinese lion dance is often mistakenly referred to as dragon dance.

C) This style of dancing is based on close observation of the lion's actual behavior.

D) The lion's head is traditionally constructed from papier-mâché and a bamboo frame.

**16**

Which choice adds a third example most similar to the examples already in the sentence?

A) NO CHANGE

B) leaping high into the air.

C) kicking our legs.

D) singing traditional songs.

**17**

A) NO CHANGE

B) tale, which originated long ago.

C) tale, and this was very old.

D) tale.

**18**

A) NO CHANGE

B) sound of drums, gongs, and cymbals,

C) sound, of drums gongs, and cymbals

D) sound of drums, gongs, and cymbals –

**19**

Which choice maintains the pattern already established in the sentence

A) NO CHANGE

B) a dynamic spiriting being symbolized by gold.

C) gold, symbolizing a dynamic spirit.

D) gold, which symbolizes a dynamic spirit.

From the movements of two people taking the head and tail to the beating of the drums, the Lion Dance is the aspect of Chinese culture I appreciate most. **20** Nevertheless, there is something magical about watching how performers can make a lion come to life. I like to think that my dancing brings good luck, happiness, and prosperity. The sights and sounds of this centuries-old tradition **21** thrill me. They give me the chance to hold on to the past while living in the present. **22** When I control the lion's head, I enjoy giving instructions to the dancers who form the lion's body.

A) NO CHANGE
B) Therefore,
C) In contrast,
D) Indeed,

A) NO CHANGE
B) thrills
C) has thrilled
D) thrilling

Which choice most logically ends the passage with a restatement of the writer's primary theme?

A) NO CHANGE
B) Last spring, I had the opportunity to perform at a very important festival.
C) One of my favorite skills to show off is a flying leap.
D) I can't help but marvel at the intricate and powerful art of lion dance.

**Questions 23-33 are based on the following passage.**

**Dolphin Talk**

In an aquarium in Hawaii, two dolphins swim in adjoining tanks. Swimming in the first tank is a mother dolphin; in the second swims her calf. While the dolphins cannot move between tanks, they can communicate via a special audio link. When the link is **23** verified, the dolphins immediately begin squawking and chirping. It seems clear that they know they are talking to each other, but less clear is what that means.

In many ways, studying dolphin communication patterns **24** pose challenges for researchers. While dolphins spend most of their lives swimming beneath the ocean's **25** waves; they are mammals and must regularly swim to the surface for air. Like people, they team up in groups – known as pods – to accomplish tasks. They also communicate verbally with one another.

**23**

A) NO CHANGE
B) activated
C) energized
D) roused

**24**

A) NO CHANGE
B) poses
C) have posed
D) having posed

**25**

A) NO CHANGE
B) waves, and they
C) waves. They
D) waves, they

**26** Dolphin "conversations" can take a variety of forms. Sometimes one dolphin will vocalize and then another will seem to answer. **27** For example, members of a pod vocalize in different patterns at the same time, creating an ear-splitting din. And just as people move their hands as they talk, dolphins communicate through gestures such as clapping their jaws and blowing bubbles.

**26**

The writer wants to link the first paragraph with the ideas that follow. Which choice best accomplishes this goal?

A) NO CHANGE
B) Dolphins maintain intricate social networks consisting of both close and casual associates.
C) Dolphins' vocalizations travel almost five times as quickly through water as through air.
D) Dolphins do not always respond immediately to other dolphins' calls, though.

**27**

A) NO CHANGE
B) Therefore
C) In other instances,
D) In fact,

Scientists think dolphins "discuss" everything from basic facts like their age to their emotional state. **28** Researchers once observed a pair of bottlenose dolphins bully a spotted dolphin. The next day, the spotted dolphin return to the scene with a pair of dolphins from his own pod, and the three **29** preceded to harass the original aggressor. It seemed evident that the spotted dolphin had communicated to his pod-mates that he needed their help **30** so that they could console him.

**28**

The writer is considering adding the following sentence.

> When dolphins get into trouble, for instance, they often call for backup.

Should the writer make this addition?

A) Yes, because it provides an effective introduction to the example that follows.

B) Yes, because it describes a particular type of sound dolphins make.

C) No, because it repeats information presented earlier in the passage.

D) No, because it presents information that is not relevant to the focus of the paragraph.

**29**

A) NO CHANGE

B) preceded in harassing

C) proceeded to harass

D) proceeded at harassing

**30**

Which choice most effectively completes the sentence with logical and relevant information.

A) NO CHANGE

B) and explained what had happened in detail.

C) in order to recover from the attack.

D) and then led them in a search for the offender.

[1] Kathleen Dudzinski, who directs the Dolphin Communication Project, **31** has listened to dolphins using high-tech equipment for more than 15 years. [2] She says, however, that she doesn't speak "dolphin" yet. [3] They are fast swimmers who can stay underwater for up to ten minutes. [4] When they appear at the surface, they remain there only briefly. [5] Almost as soon as they appear, they dive beneath the waves again. **32**

Deciphering "dolphin speak" is also challenging because the sounds dolphins make depend on whether they're playing, fighting, or seeking food. During fights, for instance, dolphins clap their jaws, but they jaw-clap while playing, too. **33** Still, researchers feel confident that someday they will solve the mystery of dolphin speech.

**31**

A) NO CHANGE

B) has used high-tech equipment to listen to dolphins for more than 15 years.

C) has spent 15 years listening to dolphins that use high-tech equipment.

D) has spent 15 years listening to dolphins using high-tech equipment.

**32**

The writer wants to add the following sentence.

Part of the reason is that dolphins are highly elusive creatures.

Where should the writer make this addition?

A) after sentence 1.

B) after sentence 2.

C) after sentence 3.

D) after sentence 4.

**33**

A) NO CHANGE

B) As such,

C) In effect,

D) For example,

**Questions 34-44 are based on the following passage.**

**It's Easy to be Green**

Driving a hybrid and recycling newspapers are ways to help conserve energy and resources. However, if you really wants to make a difference, you should take a look at the buildings **34** in which you live and work. According to the U.S. Energy Information Administration, the national organization responsible for promoting the public understanding of energy as well as its interaction with the **35** environment, and buildings account for a higher percentage of carbon dioxide emissions than either cars **36** and industry. While older structures can be retrofitted with power-saving features, specialty architects are now working to ensure that the next generation of buildings is green from the ground up. Not only are these professionals part of a growing profession but **37** he or she is also a member of the green economy.

**34**

A) NO CHANGE
B) which
C) that
D) DELETE the underlined word.

**35**

A) NO CHANGE
B) environment –
C) environment,
D) environment;

**36**

A) NO CHANGE
B) or
C) plus
D) with

**37**

A) NO CHANGE
B) you're also a member of the green economy.
C) their also members of the green economy.
D) they're also members of the green economy.

Individuals employed as sustainable architects focus on forms of building design and construction that minimize the impact of urban development on the environment. They create buildings that require less land development, use more environmentally friendly materials, and 38 contain new appliances. In addition to lessening their inhabitants' environmental footprints, these buildings can be used to teach those 39 whom live, work, or study within them about environmental issues.

Today, there is an urgent need for green architecture. Buildings represent about three-quarters of the electricity usage and half the annual energy and emissions in the United States. In some cities, the situation is even more extreme. In Philadelphia, 40 therefore, buildings generated over sixty percent of all emissions. And in New York City, 41 residential and commercial buildings were responsible for more than half of all emissions in 2009. With the built environment growing — building stock increases by about 3 billion square feet every year — architects have a historic opportunity to transform its impact for the better.

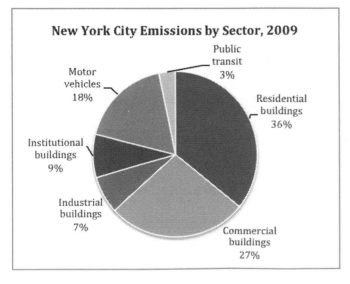

New York City Emissions by Sector, 2009

Public transit 3%
Motor vehicles 18%
Residential buildings 36%
Institutional buildings 9%
Industrial buildings 7%
Commercial buildings 27%

**38**

Which choice gives a third supporting example that is most similar to the examples already in the sentence?

A) NO CHANGE
B) are more energy efficient.
C) include outdoor spaces.
D) are fully furnished.

**39**

A) NO CHANGE
B) who live,
C) which live,
D) live,

**40**

A) NO CHANGE
B) meanwhile,
C) however,
D) for example,

**41**

A) NO CHANGE
B) commercial buildings alone were responsible for half of all emissions
C) residential buildings alone were responsible for half of all emissions
D) residential and industrial buildings were responsible for half of all emissions

There are some encouraging signs of change. Since the U.S. Green Building Council's Leadership in Energy and Environmental Design rating system appeared a dozen years ago, more than 10 billion square feet of construction have been certified or registered. **42** The average energy savings for certified buildings is around 32 percent, and over the next couple of decades, the tonnage of coal avoided is **43** estimated to grow by 16 times, according to predictions.

In response to these shifts, sustainable architecture has become an emerging specialization at many colleges and universities. A number of two- and four-year institutions, including the University of Florida, Boston Architectural College, and Kansas State University now have entire schools devoted to green construction. **44** For students with interests in a specific area of sustainability, many of these schools and programs offer concentrations such as conserving water, optimizing solar energy, or reducing the effects of construction on the environment.

Degrees and certificates in sustainable architecture are generally offered at the master's degree level; undergraduate students who plan on pursuing a career in this field can first earn bachelor's degrees in architecture or a related field, such as urban planning and design.

**42**

The writer is considering adding the following sentence.

> Architects use many different techniques to increase buildings' ability to capture or generate their own energy.

Should the writer make this addition here?

A) Yes, because it adds a relevant description of how green architects perform their jobs.
B) Yes, because it provides general background for the discussion of average energy savings.
C) No, because it interrupts the paragraph's focus on positive developments in sustainability.
D) No, because it implies that architects are not directly involved in the construction process.

**43**

A) NO CHANGE
B) estimated to grow by 16 times, and predictions say this.
C) estimated to grow by 16 times.
D) estimated to grow by a predicted 16 times.

**44**

Which choice most effectively sets up the information that follows?

A) NO CHANGE
B) Most of them encourage students to pursue multidisciplinary projects, so
C) Because they draw students from all over the world,
D) Although they were founded only recently,

**Test 4: Explanations**

1. C: Parallel structure

The other two items in the list are nouns (*an astronomer*, *a writer*), so the third item must be a noun as well. Only C contains that construction.

2. C: Comma with name

When a name appears in the middle of a sentence, it should not be preceded by a comma. (Commas before and after are acceptable, as is a comma after). That eliminates A. To check B, treat the name like any other non-essential clause and cross it out. The sentence still makes grammatical sense, but the reference to L'Enfant in the following sentence does not. The name is therefore essential, and no commas should be used. D is incorrect because a colon should be used to set off either a list or an explanation. The information that follows is neither, and the colon also breaks up the sentence unnecessarily.

3. B: Diction

The paragraph is describing L'Enfant's enthusiasm about designing the layout of Washington, D.C., a city that did not actually exist yet. In that context, the underlined word must mean something like "imagined." *Envisioned* is the closest in meaning. *Exhibited* (showed off), *imported* (brought in) and *predicted* do not make sense.

4. A: Add/delete/change

To identify the main topic of the paragraph, look at the topic sentence. What does it tell us? Building the capital was harder than expected. The only answer directly consistent with that idea is A, as indicated by the phrases *numerous delays* and *more slowly*.

5. B: Dangling modifier

Who was stubborn and short-tempered? L'Enfant. So L'Enfant, the subject, must come immediately after the comma. Only B contains that construction.

6. A: Register

Although the original version is somewhat formal (a "feat" is a difficult task), it is not excessively so. B is far too casual, and D is incorrect because Banneker did not finish an idea but rather an action (reproducing L'Enfant's plan). C can be eliminated because it is far too formal.

7. C: Add/delete/change

What does the previous sentence indicate? Banneker established an *international* reputation. The references to France and England in C are most consistent with that idea.

8. D: Sentence vs. fragment

In the original version, the inclusion of *who* after Thomas Jefferson's name creates a fragment; in C, the inclusion of *and* after *accomplishments* has the same effect. B is incorrect because a semicolon is used to separate two sentences, and the phrase before the semicolon is a fragment (*Impressed by Banneker's numerous accomplishments*). Only D correctly places a comma between the introductory clause (fragment) and the complete sentence that follows (*Thomas Jefferson, who recommended that Banneker be appointed to the surveying team responsible for lying out the city of Washington, D.C.*).

9. B: Diction

The underlined word must be a synonym for "arranging" or "planning." That is the definition of *laying out*. *Stretching out* and *elongating* both mean to physically make longer.

10. B: Transition

Start by crossing out the original transition and considering the relationship between the sentence in question and the previous question. Sentence 1: Maybe Banneker's role in reconstructing the plan has been exaggerated. Sentence 2: It's unlikely that he did the whole thing himself. Those are similar ideas, so A and C can both be eliminated. D doesn't fit since the second sentence isn't the result of the first; it simply builds on it. That leaves B, which conveys the correct relationship.

## 11. D: Paragraph order

What is the focus of paragraph 5? Benjamin Banneker's work and renown. It also mentions his appointment to the Washington D.C. planning committee. Since paragraph 4 ends by describing how Banneker reconstructed the plan – something that must have happened *after* he was appointed to the committee – paragraph 4 does not make sense where it is. A can thus be eliminated. Paragraph 4 also does not make sense after paragraph 1 because that paragraph introduces Banneker. The statement *Enter Benjamin Banneker* at the start of paragraph 4 would not be logical in that context. B can thus be eliminated. Paragraph 4 should not be placed after paragraph 2 either because that paragraph focuses only on L'Enfant's creation of the plan; it would not be logical for Banneker to be reintroduced after that. C can thus be eliminated. That leaves D, which correctly places paragraph 4 after paragraph 3. Since the end of paragraph 3 describes how L'Enfant disappeared with his plan, the paragraph 4 description of how Banneker came in and recreated the plan makes perfect sense.

## 12. B: Pronoun agreement

The underlined pronoun refers to the plural noun *dancers*, so a plural pronoun must be used. That eliminates D. *There* refers to a place, and you would not say "...I would even try to imitate they are movements," so A and C can be eliminated as well. That leaves B, which correctly provides the plural, possessive *their*.

## 13. C: Tense

The word *since* at the beginning of the sentence is a tip-off that the present perfect (*has been*) is required. C is thus the only possible option.

## 14. B: Combining sentences

A is incorrect because it is a fragment, containing gerunds (*being*, *evolving*) but no main verb. C is incorrect because it creates a dangling modifier: the phrase *First performed as a demonstration of martial arts skills* should logically modify *Lion Dancing* or *it*, not *the lion's expression*. D is incorrect because the two parts of the sentence do not really express contrasting ideas, as *but* would

indicate. In addition, the construction *the evolution to take the lion's expression and natural movements into account* is awkward and un-colloquial. That leaves B, which correctly uses the phrase *First performed as a demonstration of martial arts skills* to modify *it* (i.e. Lion Dancing).

## 15. C: Add/delete/change

What does the information following the underlined sentence indicate? That the dancers' movements are *lifelike*. Only the statement that Lion Dancing is *based on close observation of the lion's actual behavior* in C is consistent with that idea. The other choices are related to the general topic but not to the specific information that follows.

## 16. A: Parallel structure

The first two items in the list are both gerunds (*balancing*, *lifting*), so the third item must be a gerund as well (*banging*). The original version is therefore correct.

## 17. D: Redundancy, shorter is better

By definition, something ancient is very old/originated a very long time ago. Only one of those options should therefore be used.

## 18. B: Colon, commas with list

A colon must be preceded by a complete sentence that makes sense on its own, and *It thrusts its head to the sound of* is not a complete sentence. C can be eliminated because no comma should be used before a preposition (*of*). Although a single dash can be used to create a dramatic pause, there is no clear reason to place one after *cymbals*. That eliminates D. B is correct because it removes the unnecessary colon before the list and places a comma between each of the items.

## 19. C: Parallel structure

Each of the other items in the list contains the structure *color, symbolizing _____*, so the third item must contain that structure as well. Only C matches.

## 20. D: Transition

Start by crossing out the original transition and considering the relationship between the sentence in question and the previous sentence. Sentence 1: The Lion Dance is the best aspect of Chinese culture for me. Sentence 2: Making the lion come to life is magical. Those are similar ideas, so A and C can both be eliminated. B doesn't fit since the second sentence isn't actually the result of the first; it simply emphasize/builds on it. D is correct because *indeed* is used to indicate that a statement is emphasizing a point in an earlier statement.

## 21. A: Subject-verb agreement

The subject of the underlined verb is *The sights and sounds* (plural). The singular noun *tradition* is part of the prepositional phrase *of this centuries-old tradition*. A plural verb (*thrill*) is therefore required, making A correct.

## 22. D: Add/delete/change

Even if you haven't been reading the passage closely, you should be able to get the gist – the writer thinks the Lion Dance is "magical" and thrilling. (If you aren't sure, you can also go back and reread the last paragraph, which makes that theme pretty clear.) Although all of the answers are positive, D best conveys the writer's overall appreciation of the art form. The other options are too specific.

## 23. B: Diction

The correct word must mean something like "turned on." Only *activated* has that definition. *Verified* (confirmed), *energized*, and *roused* (woken up) do not fit.

## 24. B: Subject-verb agreement

The answers contain a mix of singular and plural verbs, indicating that the question is testing agreement. The subject of the underlined verb is *studying*. Gerunds are always singular when used as subjects, so a singular verb (*poses*) is required. *Pose* and *have posed* are both plural, and in D, the gerund *having* creates a fragment.

## 25. D: Semicolon, comma

A semicolon, a period, and "comma + and" are all grammatically identical, so A, B, and C can be eliminated immediately. That leaves D, which correctly places a colon between a fragment (*While dolphins spend most of their lives swimming beneath the ocean's waves*) and a sentence (*they are mammals and must regularly swim to the surface for air*).

## 26. A: Add/delete/change

What is the focus of the rest of the paragraph? The different types of dolphin "conversation" (call and response, different patterns simultaneously, gestures). Only the original version corresponds to that idea.

## 27. C: Transition

Start by crossing out the original transition and considering the relationship between the sentence in question and the previous question. Sentence 1: Sometimes one dolphin vocalizes and another one answers. Sentence 2: Dolphins make different sounds at the same time. Those are two different types of conversation, so *In other instances* creates the most logical relationship. Playing process of elimination, the second sentence isn't an example of the idea in the first sentence, nor is the second sentence the result of the first. That eliminates A and B. Since the two sentences are discussing different actions, *in fact* doesn't make sense either.

## 28. A: Add/delete/change

What does the sentence in question discuss? What happens what dolphins get into trouble. What does the paragraph discuss? It tells the story of a dolphin who got bullied (that is, got into trouble) and who got his friends to help him take revenge. Are those ideas the same or different? The same. So the sentence should be added. B can be eliminated because the sentence says nothing about the sounds dolphins make. A correctly indicates that the sentence introduces the example that follows.

## 29. C: Diction, idiom

Precede = come before; proceed = continue on. Only the second word makes sense in context. That eliminates A and B. The correct idiom is "proceed + infinitive," so C is correct.

## 30. D: Add/delete/change

Because the underlined portion of the sentence refers to the outcome of the story recounted in the paragraph, you need to back up and reread the previous couple of sentences in order to determine the answer. What happened in the story? The dolphin got his buddies, and they went and bothered the dolphin that was causing trouble. The only answer consistent with those events is D.

## 31. B: Misplaced modifier

Although the intended meaning of the original version is clear, it actually implies that the dolphins were the ones using high-tech equipment. C and D create the same problem. Only B makes it clear that Dudzinski was the one using high-tech equipment.

## 32. B: Sentence order

The phrase *Part of the reason* at the beginning of the sentence to be added indicates that the sentence is providing an explanation. It must therefore follow a sentence that requires an explanation. The only sentence after which that statement makes sense is sentence 2. The fact that dolphins are *highly elusive creatures* explains why Dudzinski still doesn't speak "dolphin" after 15 years of listening.

## 33. A: Transition

Start by crossing out the original transition and considering the relationship between the sentence in question and the previous question. Sentence 1: It's hard to figure out what dolphins are "saying" because dolphins' sounds change depending on their activity. Sentence 2: Researchers are confident they'll figure it out eventually. Those are opposing ideas, so a contradictor is required. *Still* (synonym for *however* and *nevertheless*) is the only contradictor, so A is correct. *For example*

clearly does not make sense. *As such* means "as something is," and *in effect* means "essentially," neither of which fits.

## 34. A: Pronoun

Although it may sound odd to you, the construction *in which* is perfectly acceptable and can be used interchangeably with *where*. Neither *which* or *that* fits in this context, and the sentence makes no sense if the pronoun is removed entirely.

## 35. C: Non-essential clause

This is an extremely long sentence, so be careful. To figure out what's going on, you need to back up four lines, to *According to...* If you read the sentence from the beginning, you'll find that the comma after *Administration* sets off an extremely long non-essential clause (*the national organization responsible for promoting the public understanding of energy as well as its interaction with the environment*). If you cross out the non-essential clause, the error becomes clear: *According to the U.S. Energy Information Administration ... and buildings account for a higher percentage of carbon dioxide emissions than either cars or industry*. The simplest way to correct the error is simply to remove the word *and*. That gives you C. A comma rather than a dash must be used because a comma is used at the start of the non-essential clause.

## 36. B: Word pair

*Either* should be paired only with *or*.

## 37. D: Pronoun agreement, noun agreement

The underlined noun refers to the plural noun *professionals*, so the plural pronoun *they* and the plural noun *members* must be used. That eliminates A and B. C is incorrect because you would say "they are members of the green economy;" the pronoun is not possessive. That leaves D, which correctly provides both the plural pronoun and the plural noun.

**38. B: Add/delete/change**

What is the point of the examples already in the sentence? To indicate specific aspects of sustainable buildings that are beneficial to the environment. Energy efficiency is most consistent with that idea, making B correct.

**39. B: Who vs. whom**

*Who*, not *whom*, should come before a verb, and *live* is a verb. That makes the answer B. *Which* is for things, eliminating C, and D is incorrect because removing the pronoun creates a nonsensical construction.

**40. D: Transition**

Even though the transition doesn't appear as the first word in the sentence, it's still being used to connect the sentence in which it appears to the previous sentence. Treat this question as you would any other transition question: cross out the transition, and determine the relationship between this sentence and the previous sentence. Sentence 1: Buildings in some cities use an outrageous amount of energy. Sentence 2: Buildings in Philadelphia were responsible for 60% of emissions. Since Philadelphia is a specific example of a city, *for example* is the most logical transition.

**41. A: Graphic**

A correctly states that residential and commercial buildings combined made up more than half of all emissions (a total of 63%). B is also incorrect because commercial buildings are only responsible for 27% of emissions. C is incorrect because the graph indicates that residential buildings are only responsible for 36% of emissions – less than half. D is incorrect because residential and industrial buildings combined still only make up 43%.

**42. C: Add/delete/change**

What is the focus of the sentence to be added? The fact that green architects do a variety of things to make buildings more energy-efficient. What is the focus of the paragraph? The fact that green architecture is gaining popularity. Are those two ideas the same? No. So the sentence should not be added because it is off-topic, making C correct.

**43. C: Redundancy, shorter is better**

Since *estimates* and *predictions* have the same essential meaning here, only one should be used.

**44. A: Add/delete/change**

What type of information follows? Examples of areas of green architecture in which students can specialize. The phrase *specific area* in A indicates that the original version is correct. All of the other answers are related to studying green architecture but do not clearly introduce the information that follows.

# Test 5 Answer Sheet

1. Ⓐ Ⓑ Ⓒ Ⓓ
2. Ⓐ Ⓑ Ⓒ Ⓓ
3. Ⓐ Ⓑ Ⓒ Ⓓ
4. Ⓐ Ⓑ Ⓒ Ⓓ
5. Ⓐ Ⓑ Ⓒ Ⓓ
6. Ⓐ Ⓑ Ⓒ Ⓓ
7. Ⓐ Ⓑ Ⓒ Ⓓ
8. Ⓐ Ⓑ Ⓒ Ⓓ
9. Ⓐ Ⓑ Ⓒ Ⓓ
10. Ⓐ Ⓑ Ⓒ Ⓓ
11. Ⓐ Ⓑ Ⓒ Ⓓ
12. Ⓐ Ⓑ Ⓒ Ⓓ
13. Ⓐ Ⓑ Ⓒ Ⓓ
14. Ⓐ Ⓑ Ⓒ Ⓓ
15. Ⓐ Ⓑ Ⓒ Ⓓ
16. Ⓐ Ⓑ Ⓒ Ⓓ
17. Ⓐ Ⓑ Ⓒ Ⓓ
18. Ⓐ Ⓑ Ⓒ Ⓓ
19. Ⓐ Ⓑ Ⓒ Ⓓ
20. Ⓐ Ⓑ Ⓒ Ⓓ
21. Ⓐ Ⓑ Ⓒ Ⓓ
22. Ⓐ Ⓑ Ⓒ Ⓓ

23. Ⓐ Ⓑ Ⓒ Ⓓ
24. Ⓐ Ⓑ Ⓒ Ⓓ
25. Ⓐ Ⓑ Ⓒ Ⓓ
26. Ⓐ Ⓑ Ⓒ Ⓓ
27. Ⓐ Ⓑ Ⓒ Ⓓ
28. Ⓐ Ⓑ Ⓒ Ⓓ
29. Ⓐ Ⓑ Ⓒ Ⓓ
30. Ⓐ Ⓑ Ⓒ Ⓓ
31. Ⓐ Ⓑ Ⓒ Ⓓ
32. Ⓐ Ⓑ Ⓒ Ⓓ
33. Ⓐ Ⓑ Ⓒ Ⓓ
34. Ⓐ Ⓑ Ⓒ Ⓓ
35. Ⓐ Ⓑ Ⓒ Ⓓ
36. Ⓐ Ⓑ Ⓒ Ⓓ
37. Ⓐ Ⓑ Ⓒ Ⓓ
38. Ⓐ Ⓑ Ⓒ Ⓓ
39. Ⓐ Ⓑ Ⓒ Ⓓ
40. Ⓐ Ⓑ Ⓒ Ⓓ
41. Ⓐ Ⓑ Ⓒ Ⓓ
42. Ⓐ Ⓑ Ⓒ Ⓓ
43. Ⓐ Ⓑ Ⓒ Ⓓ
44. Ⓐ Ⓑ Ⓒ Ⓓ

# Writing and Language Test
## 35 MINUTES, 44 QUESTIONS

**Turn to Section 2 of your answer sheet to answer the questions in this section.**

**DIRECTIONS**

Each passage below is accompanied by a number of questions. For some questions, you will consider how the passage might be revised to improve the expression of ideas. For other questions, you will consider how the passage might be edited to correct errors in sentence structure, usage, or punctuation. A passage or a question may be accompanied by one or more graphics (such as a table or graph) that you will consider as you make revising and editing decisions.

Some questions will direct you to an underlined portion of a passage. Other questions will direct you to a location in a passage or ask you to think about the passage as a whole.

After reading each passage, choose the answer to each question that most effectively improves the quality of writing in the passage or that makes the passage conform to the conventions of standard written English. Many questions include a "NO CHANGE" option. Choose that option if you think the best choice is to leave the relevant portion of the passage as it is.

**Questions 1-11 are based on the following passage.**

**Superflat**

When Takashi Murakami was a young artist, he observed that Japanese art was beginning to lose some of **1** it's unique qualities. For centuries, Japanese painters had emphasized flat, two-dimensional images in their work. Even as a student, however, Murakami observed that three dimensional western-style figures were growing more common. **2** Much of his early work was done in the spirit of social criticism and mockery.

**1**

A) NO CHANGE
B) its
C) his
D) their

**2**

The writer wants to link the first paragraph with the ideas that follow. Which choice best accomplishes this goal?

A) NO CHANGE
B) He was inspired by these works and wanted to imitate them.
C) This shift reflected changes in Japanese culture.
D) Concerned by this development, he went on to found the superflat movement.

Works produced in this style combine the principles of traditional Japanese art with those of 1950s Japanese pop culture images. As a result, superflat painting is an intriguing blend of classical and modern that **3** have made Murakami one of the most important artists of his generation.

Murakami, who was born and raised in Tokyo, developed a strong interest in manga (Japanese comics) at an early age. As a child, he **4** inspired to someday work in the animation industry. When he entered the Tokyo University of the Arts, his goal was to obtain the skills necessary to work an animator; however, he later changed his mind and decided to major in Nihonga **5** . Murakami went on to earn a doctorate in Nihonga, but he eventually found himself drawn back to more contemporary forms of art. His early pieces were often **6** satirical. They poked fun at his fellow artists' tendency to automatically copy western styles.

**3**

A) NO CHANGE
B) has made
C) having made
D) make

**4**

A) NO CHANGE
B) transpired
C) perspired
D) aspired

**5**

The writer is considering adding the following information.

   – the classical painting style that incorporates traditional Japanese conventions, techniques, and subjects.

Should the writer make this addition?

A) Yes, because it explains a term that readers are likely to be unfamiliar with.
B) Yes, because it illustrates why Murakami decided not to work as an animator.
C) No, because it does not support the idea that Murakami was interested in contemporary art.
D) No, because it distorts the paragraphs focus on Murakami's childhood.

**6**

What is the best way to combine the sentences at the underlined portion?

A) satirical; and they poked fun
B) satirical, they poked fun
C) satirical and poke fun
D) satirical, poking fun

In 1994, the Asian Cultural Council awarded Murakami a fellowship that allowed him to spend a year in New York, where he established a small studio. When he returned to Japan, he further developed his artistic vision and **7** beginning to exhibit his work at galleries and museums in Europe and the United States.

Six years later, Murakami published his "Superflat" theory in the catalogue for a group exhibition that he curated for the Museum of Contemporary Art in Los Angeles. He suggested that unlike western art, which emphasizes realistic surfaces and flat planes of **8** color, while Japanese art is based on "flat" two-dimensional imagery that can still be observed in manga and anime (animated works). **9** However, Murakami used exhibits such as "Coloriage" and "Little Boy" to elaborate on this theory, which became a central part of his artistic practice.

In addition to exhibiting his work in well-known venues, Murakami uses his art for more practical goals. **10** He has, for example, used his works to introduce Japan's creative culture to audiences around the world. He also attempts to **11** scrape the distinction between popular art and "high" art by repackaging his "high-art" works as merchandise such as stuffed animals and T-shirts and making them available at affordable prices.

**7**

A) NO CHANGE
B) has begun
C) began
D) will begin

**8**

A) NO CHANGE
B) color – Japanese
C) color, Japanese
D) color; Japanese

**9**

A) NO CHANGE
B) Consequently, Murakami
C) Meanwhile, Murakami
D) Murakami

**10**

Which choice best supports the statement made in the previous sentence?

A) NO CHANGE
B) In September, 2010 Murakami became the third contemporary artist to exhibit his works at the Palace of Versailles in France.
C) In fact, his work has continued to rise in value and can sell for millions of dollars.
D) In contrast, the exhibition Murakami-Ego exhibition showcased around 60 old works alongside new ones.

**11**

A) NO CHANGE
B) scribble
C) erase
D) delay

**Questions 12-22 are based on the following passage.**

**Lucky Lindy**

In 1919, the hotel baron Raymond Orteig made an offer that was hard to **12** refuse: he would award $25,000 to any pilot who could successfully fly from New York to Paris within five years. Unfortunately, aviation technology in the early 1920s was still very crude. **13** Born in the south of France, Orteig decided to renew the challenge for an additional five-year period. The second round of the contest attracted an impressive group of well-known and highly experienced **14** contenders, however, it did not produce a winner.

In the mid-1920s, Charles Lindbergh was an obscure Air Mail pilot who delivered packages between Chicago and St. Louis. From an early age, he exhibited an interest in the mechanics of motorized transportation. As a college student studying mechanical engineering, he became fascinated with flying **15** when he had never so much as touched an airplane. After leaving college in 1922, Lindbergh enrolled at the Nebraska Aircraft Corporation's flying school, ultimately earning his certification as a flight instructor.

**12**

A) NO CHANGE
B) refuse, he would award $25,000
C) refuse, he would award $25,000,
D) refuse; he would award $25,000 –

**13**

Which choice most effectively sets up the information that follows?

A) NO CHANGE
B) When no winner emerged,
C) A supporter of numerous charitable activities,
D) Having worked his way up in the hotel industry

**14**

A) NO CHANGE
B) contenders, so it did not produce
C) contenders but not producing
D) contenders; it did not, however, produce

**15**

A) NO CHANGE
B) since
C) even though
D) despite

When Lindbergh entered Orteig's competition, he faced several major challenges. First, he lacked the kind of sponsorship that some of his competitors had. **[16]** In fact, he started out with only $2,000 of his own savings and his $350 monthly salary from U.S. Air Mail. Eventually, though, he was able to obtain the backing of two prominent St. Louis businessmen, Harry Knight and Harold Bixby. With their help, Lindberg managed to **[17]** secure a loan large enough to fund the project. The next problem was finding a plane. The men attempted to purchase a suitable aircraft from several large manufacturers, but **[18]** the costs were excessively high. Lindbergh intended to pilot the plane himself, so he was forced to search for another option.

**16**

The writer is considering deleting the underlined sentence. Should the writer do this?

A) Yes, because it distorts the focus of the passage by focusing on Lindbergh's finances rather than his flying skills.

B) Yes, because it does not provide a comparison between Lindbergh's finances and those of his competitors.

C) No, because it provides a specific illustration of the primary claim of the paragraph.

D) No, because it explains how Lindbergh was able to attract prominent backers.

**17**

A) NO CHANGE

B) latch onto

C) seize

D) rustle up

**18**

Which choice most effectively sets up the contrast in the sentence and is consistent with the information in the rest of the passage?

A) NO CHANGE

B) all of them insisted on choosing the pilot.

C) the engines were not strong enough for such a long flight.

D) they could not agree on the specifications.

Finally, the group turned to Ryan Aircraft Company, a smaller manufacturer in San Diego whose owner, B.F. Mahoney, **19** agreeing to build a single-engine plane to Lindbergh's specifications. The contract was signed on February 25, 1927. Dubbed "The Spirit of St. Louis," the plane made its first flight just over two months later. After completing a series of test flights, Lindbergh first flew to St. Louis; **20** subsequently, he traveled to Garden City, New York. He took off from Roosevelt field on May 20th, arriving in France the next morning. Not only had he traveled over 3,500 hundred miles across the Atlantic Ocean **21** but also to become the first person ever to stand in North America one day and in Europe the next.

**22** Immediately, the 25 year-old pilot became an instant celebrity worldwide. Newspaper headlines on both sides of the Atlantic announced "Lucky Lindy's" achievement to the world. For his historic exploit, Lindbergh was also awarded the United States' highest military decoration: the Medal of Honor.

**19**

A) NO CHANGE
B) who agreed
C) agreed
D) agrees

**20**

A) NO CHANGE
B) however,
C) meanwhile,
D) hence,

**21**

A) NO CHANGE
B) but also becoming
C) but he had also become
D) and he also became

**22**

A) NO CHANGE
B) The 25 year-old pilot became an instant celebrity
C) The 25 year-old pilot immediately became an instant celebrity
D) The 25 year-old pilot became an instant celebrity right away

**Questions 23-33 are based on the following passage.**

**Open Office**

For most of the twentieth century, workplaces were designed with long hallways containing rows of offices or cramped cubicles; however, in recent years, office layouts have shifted to open-plan models **23** that are more cost-effective. Today, almost 70% of all business in the United States have open offices.

From a philosophical perspective, glass walls and a lack of barriers between workers represent transparency and flexibility. **24** Practically speaking, open floor plans reflect the fact that paper usage has been reduced. Most correspondence is now sent electronically, making mailrooms a thing of the past. Likewise, most documents are now stored on computers, so room for bulky file cabinets **25** is no longer needed.

Which choice most logically completes the description of open-plan models and provides the best introduction to the passage?

A) NO CHANGE
B) with long tables where employees can interact freely.
C) that are implemented after discussion with senior executives.
D) that some employees initially resist.

## 24

Which choice best maintains the sentence pattern established in the paragraph?

A) NO CHANGE
B) In a practical sense, open floor plans reflect the fact of paper usage having been reduced.
C) From a practical perspective, open floor plans reflect a decreased need for paper.
D) Considering things practically, reduced paper usage is reflected in open floor plans.

A) NO CHANGE
B) are
C) would be
D) being

Open-plan environments also provide more opportunities for collaboration, both planned and spontaneous, as well as a greater sense of community. According to a study in *Harvard Business Review*, employees at companies that switched to open offices were more than four times as productive – **26** otherwise, faster and more accurate – as those that remained in closed ones.

One company that has managed the transition to open offices especially well is Clif Bar® & **27** Company. Which is a leading maker of organic sports nutrition foods and healthy snacks. Members of the design team explored every aspect of the company, attempting to get a personal feel for its culture and community through guided tours, focus groups, and **28** employee interviews. The insights they gained allowed them to **29** restrain the essence of the Clif Bar brand when they built the business's new offices.

**26**

A) NO CHANGE
B) however,
C) in reality,
D) that is,

**27**

A) NO CHANGE
B) Company; which is a leading maker
C) Company, it is a leading maker
D) Company, a leading maker

**28**

Which choice gives a third supporting example that is most similar to the examples already in the sentence?

A) NO CHANGE
B) press releases.
C) promotional materials.
D) financial data.

**29**

A) NO CHANGE
B) capture
C) tie up
D) hold down

The 75,000 square-foot facility, which opened in Emeryville, California in 2010, transformed an original World War II valve manufacturing facility into a workplace haven for the company's outdoor enthusiasts. The space celebrates the inherent natural light of a repurposed warehouse while using a series of interior gardens to connect employees to the outdoors. **30** Designers often drew by hand or navigated the digital model of the project live in front of workers to illustrate ideas in real time.

Unfortunately, Clif Bar's success may be the exception rather than the rule. A study conducted by the University of Sydney found that **31** workers in open offices were significantly more satisfied with their visual privacy, sound privacy, and noise levels than those in private offices.

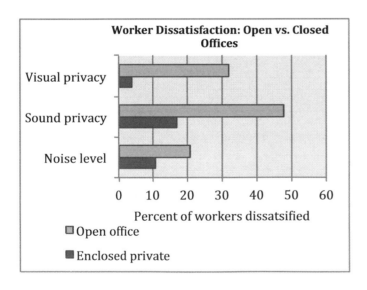

**30**

At this point, the writer wants to add specific information that supports the main topic of the paragraph.

A) NO CHANGE

B) In addition, the building features a cafeteria, a movie theater, a childcare facility, and an exercise room.

C) Doors feature custom handles made from bicycle frames, and solar panels line the roof.

D) On the upstairs level, an additional mezzanine and walkway increase the workstation capacity.

**31**

Which choice accurately reflects the data presented in the graph?

A) NO CHANGE

B) workers in open offices were slightly more satisfied with their visual privacy, sound privacy, and noise levels than were workers in private offices.

C) workers in open offices were significantly less satisfied with their visual privacy, sound privacy, and noise level than were workers in private offices

D) workers in open offices were slightly less satisfied with their visual privacy, sound privacy, and noise level than were workers in private offices

Other studies have shown that moving employees from closed to open spaces works best if the need **32** with privacy is recognized and accommodated. Companies can address this challenge by providing what are often referred to as "short-stay rooms" or "telephone rooms." These are usually small, private rooms where workers can spend a few hours making private calls or doing heads-down work **33** where he or she requires privacy. Companies are still experimenting with ways to balance their employees' needs, but open offices in some form are probably here to stay.

**32**

A) NO CHANGE
B) to
C) for
D) in

**33**

A) NO CHANGE
B) where privacy is required by them.
C) in which one requires privacy.
D) that requires privacy.

**Questions 34-44 are based on the following passage.**

**The Exercise Pill**

It doesn't seem right that a simple drug should allow people to avoid the pain and sweat that accompany the pursuit of a ▮34▮ lean, fit body, but new scientific developments suggest that what was once the stuff of mid-workout fantasies may soon be reality. Researchers have repeatedly tried to identify the molecular processes that occur when we exercise and the positive effects on our ▮35▮ cells in recent months, they have made progress in observing how these processes function. That knowledge could someday lead to the development of an "exercise pill."

▮36▮ According recent studies, over 80% of people in the United States do not get the recommended amount of exercise. Researchers recruited a group of healthy non-athletes, who were asked to engage in high-intensity workouts for 10 minutes. After ▮37▮ he or she was done exercising, the scientists used a technique called mass spectrometry to analyze how the exercise had affected protein activity in the subjects' cells. The results indicated that exercise causes around 1,000 molecular ▮38▮ changes, most of them had never been associated with exercise. Still, the findings provided the first clear blueprint of how exercise affects cells.

**34**

A) NO CHANGE
B) lean, fit, body, but
C) lean, fit body, however
D) lean fit, body, but

**35**

A) NO CHANGE
B) cells, in recent months,
C) cells. In recent months,
D) cells in recent months

**36**

Which choice provides the most effective introduction to the paragraph?

A) NO CHANGE
B) One recent study led to a breakthrough in understanding what happens inside people's bodies when they exercise.
C) After declining throughout the early 2000s, exercise rates are now beginning to improve.
D) Nearly 75% of people in the United States that they engage in sustained exercise at least once a week.

**37**

A) NO CHANGE
B) one was
C) these guys were
D) the subjects were

**38**

A) NO CHANGE
B) changes, most of them never being
C) changes. Most of which had never been
D) changes, most of which had never been

Other findings are even more promising. A team of scientists at the University of Southampton in Great Britain created a molecule named "Compound 14." It works by setting off a chemical reaction that "tricks" cells into thinking they need **39** energy. As a result, there is an increase in their metabolism. The researchers gave Compound 14 to a group of mice that had been fed a high-fat diet. The mice were obese and glucose intolerant – signs of pre-diabetes. **40** After consuming a single dose, their blood glucose level dropped to near normal. Then, the mice were divided into two groups: both groups were fed the same diet, but the first group was given a single dose of Compound 14 every day for a week, while the second group was given an inactive compound. At the end of a week, **41** the mice that received Compound 14 had lost around seven grams, while those receiving the inactive compound had lost the same amount.

**39**

What is the most effective way of combining the sentences at the underlined portion?

A) energy, thereby increasing
B) energy, consequently an increase is created in
C) energy, therefore there is an increase in
D) energy, so an increase occurring in

**40**

A) NO CHANGE
B) After the mice consumed a single dose,
C) Having consumed a single dose
D) In consuming a single dose,

**41**

At this point, the writer wants to add specific information that supports the main topic of the paragraph.

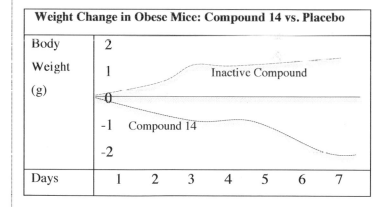

| Weight Change in Obese Mice: Compound 14 vs. Placebo | | | | | | | | |
|---|---|---|---|---|---|---|---|---|
| Body Weight (g) | 2 | | | | | | | |
| | 1 | | Inactive Compound | | | | | |
| | 0 | | | | | | | |
| | -1 | Compound 14 | | | | | | |
| | -2 | | | | | | | |
| Days | | 1 | 2 | 3 | 4 | 5 | 6 | 7 |

A) NO CHANGE
B) the mice that received Compound 14 had gained around seven grams, while those receiving the inactive compound lost two grams.
C) the mice that received Compound 14 had lost around two grams, while those receiving the inactive compound gained more than one gram.
D) the mice that received Compound 14 had lost around two grams, while those receiving the inactive compound had gained more than two grams.

Researchers hope to develop Compound 14 and analyze [42] its long-term effects. If it works in humans, it could become a way to treat both obesity and Type 2 Diabetes, both of which are widespread in the United States population. [43] Researchers also believe that exercise pills could strongly benefit [44] people, who have sustained injuries, as well as those born with physical limitations. For most of us, though, no pill will provide all the benefits of real exercise – at least not for the foreseeable future.

**42**

A) NO CHANGE
B) its long-term effects'.
C) it's long-term effects.
D) their long-term effects.

**43**

The writer is considering adding the following sentence.

> Currently more than one-third (78.6 million) of adults are obese and over 25 million people have Type 2 Diabetes.

Should the writer make this addition here?

A) Yes, because it explains what the writer means by "widespread."
B) Yes, because it calls attention to the long-term effects of Compound 14.
C) No, because it does not support the claim that Compound 14 may have more benefits for mice than for humans.
D) No, because it does not explain how Compound 14's effectiveness will be tested in humans.

**44**

A) NO CHANGE
B) people, who have sustained injuries
C) people; who have sustained injuries
D) people who have sustained injuries

**Test 5: Explanations**

1. B: Pronoun agreement

The underlined pronoun most logically refers to the singular noun *Japanese art*. Since you would not say "…Japanese art was beginning to lose it is unique qualities," the possessive *its* is correct. Its = the unique qualities of Japanese art.

2. D: Add/delete/change

To answer this question, you must jump ahead to the next page and read the following paragraph. The references to *this style* and *superflat painting* indicate that the correct answer must be related to Murakami's style. Only D, which mentions the superflat movement, is consistent with that idea.

3. D: Subject-verb agreement

The presence of both singular and plural answer choices indicates that this question is testing agreement; the inclusion of different tense is a distraction. The subject of the underlined verb is the singular noun *an intriguing blend*. A singular verb is thus required. *Have made* and *make* are both plural, and *having* creates a fragment. That leaves B, which correctly includes the singular verb *has*.

4. D: Diction

*Aspired* (aimed, strove) is the only word that fits in context. *Inspired*, *transpired* (occurred), and *perspired* (sweated) all do not make sense.

5. A: Add/delete/change

What is the focus of the information to be added? It's basically a description of a classical painting style. What is the focus of the sentence that it would be added onto? The fact that Murakami decided to study Nihonga. Does the information belong? Yes, because it defines Nihonga, a term readers are unlikely to be familiar with.

6. D: Combining sentences

A is incorrect because *and* should only follow a comma, not a semicolon. B is incorrect because

the construction "comma + they" signals a comma splice. C is incorrect because it contains an unnecessary tense switch (*poke* is in the present, whereas the rest of the paragraph is in the past). D correctly places a comma between a complete sentence and the fragment that modifies it.

7. C: Parallel structure

The word *and* indicates that the underlined verb is paired with the past tense verb *developed*, so the underlined verb must be in the past tense as well. That makes *began* the only option.

8. C: Non-essential clause

If you back up to the beginning of the sentence, you can see that the comma after *art* marks the beginning of a non-essential clause. If that clause is removed, the error becomes clear. *He suggested that unlike western art…while Japanese art is based on "flat" two-dimensional imagery that can still be observed in manga and anime (animated works)*. The simplest way to correct the sentence is to eliminate the word *while*. A comma must mark the end of the non-essential clause because it marks the beginning of the clause.

9. D: Transition

Start by crossing out the original transition and considering the relationship between the sentence in question and the previous sentence. Sentence 1: Murakami believed that western art = 3D, Japanese art = flat. Sentence 2: His work reflects that idea. Those are similar ideas, so A can be eliminated. The second sentence is not the result of the first, so B can be eliminated. *Meanwhile* simply makes no sense in this context. That leaves D, which is correct. There is no reason to place a transition between the sentences.

10. A: Add/delete/change

What is the point of the previous sentence? Murakami uses his art for practical purposes. The original version lists some things Murakami attempts to do with his art. If you're not sure, though, check the other answers. B talks about an achievement, not a practical goal. C focuses on the monetary value of Murakami's art, but that has nothing to do with practical goals. D does not make sense in context; there's absolutely no contrast with the previous sentence. So that again leaves A.

## 11. C: Diction

In context of the fact that Murakami tries to turn his "high" art into popular merchandise, the underlined word must mean something like "eliminates." The only word with that meaning is *erase*.

## 12. A: Colon, comma splice

The original version correctly uses a colon to set up the explanation of Orteig's offer. B and C can be eliminated because they contain comma splices (signaled by "comma + he"), and D is incorrect because there is no logical reason to break up the sentence with a dash after $25,000.

## 13. B: Add/delete/change

What is the focus of the information that follows? Orteig renewed the contest to find someone who could fly across the Atlantic. Why would he do that? Because no one managed to do so successfully the first time. The only answer consistent with that idea is B: Orteig *renewed the challenge* because there was no winner.

## 14. D: Transition, comma

*However* can be used in two ways: non-essentially (comma before and after) or at the start of a sentence (after a semicolon/period). The original version uses *however* non-essentially. To check it out, cross out the word and read the sentence without it: *The second round of the contest attracted an impressive group of well-known and highly experienced contenders…it did not produce a winner.* No, that doesn't work – now there's no punctuation between the two sentences, and a run-on is created. Although B is grammatically acceptable, it is also wrong because *so* indicates a cause-and-effect relationship. C is incorrect because a conjugated verb rather than a gerund (*producing*) is required. D is correct because it places a semicolon between the two sentences and retains the word *however*, using it non-essentially.

While that placement may seem odd to you, it works grammatically. When *however* is crossed out, the sentence still makes sense (*it did not… produce a winner*).

## 15. C: Transition

Start by considering the information before and after the transition. Part 1: Lindbergh became fascinated with flying. Part 2: He had never touched an airplane. Those are contrasting ideas, so a contradictor is required. Both *even though* and *despite* are contradictors, but the latter does not fit grammatically (*despite* must be followed by a noun).

## 16. C: Add/delete/change

Start by reading the paragraph, or at least everything from the beginning until a sentence or two after the underlined sentence. What is the focus of the paragraph? The "major challenges" that Lindbergh faced. What is the focus of the underlined sentence? Lindberg didn't have a lot of money starting out. Are those two ideas consistent? Yes. The underlined sentence supports the main idea of the paragraph. So it should be kept, and the answer is C.

## 17. A: Diction

*Secure a loan* is a fixed idiomatic phrase meaning "obtain a loan."

## 18. B: Add/delete/change

Although this question refers to the rest of the passage, start by focusing on the information immediately surrounding the underlined portion. The following sentence states that Lindbergh searched for another option because he *intended to pilot the plane himself*. That means that the large manufacturers must have wanted someone else to pilot the plane. That is what B indicates, so it is the correct answer. Although the other answers form contrasts with the first half of the sentence, they do not fit in logically with the information that follows.

19. C: Sentence vs. fragment, parallel structure

In the original version, the use of a gerund (*agreeing*) rather than a verb creates a fragment; there is no main verb. The inclusion of *who* before the verb in B creates the same problem – the verb "belongs" to *who* rather than to its actual subject, *B.F. Mahoney*. In order for the statement to be a sentence, a verb must be used right after the comma. The verb must also be parallel to the surrounding past-tense verbs (*turned*, *was*, *made*). That makes C, *agreed*, the only option.

20. A: Transition

Start by crossing out the original transition and considering the relationship between the two halves of the sentence. Part 1: Lindbergh flew to St. Louis after a bunch of test flights. Part 2: He flew to Garden City. That is a sequence of events. The only transition consistent with that idea is *subsequently*, meaning "next." Playing process of elimination, B can be eliminated because there is no contradiction, and D can be eliminated because the second action did not result from the first. C, *meanwhile*, does not fit because Lindbergh could not have traveled to St. Louis and Garden City simultaneously.

21. C: Word pair, parallel structure

Because *not only* appears, *but also* must appear as well. That eliminates D. The construction after *but also* must be the same as it is after *not only*. *Not only* is followed by "had + verb," so *but also* must be followed by the same. That makes C correct.

22. B: Redundancy, shorter is better

*Immediately*, *instant*, and *right away* have the same meaning. Only one of those options should be used.

23. B: Add/delete/change

The introduction itself doesn't give you much to go on, but the topic sentence of the second paragraph tells you what you need to know. *Transparency*, *flexibility*, and a *lack of barriers* directly correspond to the idea of interacting freely, making B correct.

24. C: Parallel structure

The previous sentence begins with the phrase *From a philosophical perspective*, so the second sentence must follow that template and begin with *From a _____ perspective*. Only C contains that construction.

25. A: Subject-verb agreement

The subject of the underlined verb is the singular noun *room*; the plural noun *cabinets*, which immediately precedes the verb, is part of the prepositional phrase *for bulky file cabinets*. A singular verb is therefore required, making the original version correct. B is incorrect because *are* is plural; C contains an unnecessary tense switch; and the gerund *being* in D creates a fragment.

26. D: Transition

The easiest way to answer this question is to recognize that dashes are often used to set up explanations or definitions. In this case, the phrase *faster and more accurate* is used to define what is meant by "productive." The transition used to introduce explanations is *that is*, making the answer D. Otherwise, you can play process of elimination. *Faster and more accurate* is consistent with the idea of productivity, so a contradictor should not be used. That eliminates A and B. *In reality* is used to emphasize that something is not what it appears to be, so C does not make sense either. Again, that leaves A.

27. D: Sentence vs. fragment

A period and a semicolon are grammatically identical, so A and B can both be eliminated immediately. (In addition, a sentence should not begin with *which*, as is the case in B.) In C, the construction "comma + it" signals a comma splice, making that answer incorrect as well. D correctly uses a comma to separate a complete sentence (*One company that has managed the transition to open offices especially well is Clif Bar & Company*) from the fragment that modifies it (*a leading maker of organic sports nutrition foods and healthy snacks*).

28. A: Add/delete/change

What is the point of the examples already in the sentence? To illustrate how the design team attempted to get a *personal* understanding of Clif Bar's company culture. The example most consistent with that idea is *employee interviews*. The other options are less personal.

29. B: Diction

The correct idiom is "capture the essence." The other options have literal meanings related to the idea of capturing but are not idiomatically correct.

30. C: Add/delete/change

To identify the main topic of the paragraph, back up to the topic sentence. What does it indicate? The new offices were transformed into *a work haven for* <u>outdoor enthusiasts</u>. The correct answer must be consistent with that idea. C is correct because *bicycle frames* and *solar panels* are both items related to the outdoors. The other options are related to the offices as a whole but not specifically to the outdoors.

31. C: Graphic

Since the answers contain a good deal of information, start by summarizing the graph. The information below the graph indicates that it represents the percent of workers who are *dissatisfied*. In other word, long bar = unhappy workers. The light gray bar represents open offices, and the dark gray bar represents traditional offices. Although there is some variation, the light gray bar is notably longer than the dark gray bar at each point of comparison. That indicates that workers in open offices were much more dissatisfied, i.e. much LESS satisfied than workers in traditional offices. That makes the answer C.

32. C: Preposition, idiom

The correct idiom is "need for." A preposition other than *for* should not be used.

33. D: Pronoun agreement, relative pronoun

Although the pronoun *where* in A and B can be understood to refer to short-stay rooms, that noun appears much earlier in the sentence. Normally, *where* should be placed immediately after the noun (place) to which it refers. Here, however, the noun immediately before *where* is *work* – in this context an activity, not a place. That eliminates A and B. In addition, A contains a disagreement between the plural noun *workers* and the singular pronoun *he or she*, and B is awkward and passive. C is incorrect because *one* must be paired with *one*. D correctly uses *that* to refer to work and employs the shortest, clearest construction.

34. A: Commas with list, FANBOYS

The original version correctly places commas between the items in the list as well as before the FANBOYS conjunction *but*. B and D incorrectly place a comma between an adjective and the noun it modifies (*fit, body*). C is incorrect because *however* should follow a semicolon when it begins a clause. D is also incorrect because *lean* and *fit* must be separated by a comma.

35. C: Combining and separating sentences

If you back up and read the entire sentence, you will find that there are actually two sentences that must be broken up. A period or semicolon is therefore required. Since C is the only option to contain either, it must be correct – it simply moves the prepositional phrase *in recent months* from the end of the first sentence to the beginning of the second. Otherwise, the construction "comma + they" in the original version signals a comma splice. B is incorrect because the comma before *in* creates a comma splice. D places no punctuation between the sentences, again creating a run-on.

36. B: Add/delete/change

Start by reading the rest of the paragraph to determine its focus. What does it discuss? Research on the effects of exercise on cells. The only answer consistent with that focus is B, which refers to a study. The other answers are related to exercise, but not to the research described in the paragraph.

### 37. D: Pronoun agreement, register

The underlined pronoun refers to the plural noun *non-athletes*. A plural pronoun (*they*) is therefore required. *One* is singular, eliminating B. Although *those guys* is plural, it is also too informal. That leaves D, which correctly supplies the plural noun *subjects*.

### 38. D: Sentence vs. fragment, comma splice

The phrase *most of them* is the subject of a new sentence. As a result, the comma in the original version creates a comma splice. B is incorrect because the gerund *being* creates an awkward construction. C is incorrect because *most of which* cannot be the subject of a sentence. As a result, a statement that begins with that construction should only follow a comma, not a period (or a semicolon). That leaves D, which correctly places a comma between a complete sentence (*The results indicated that exercise causes around 1,000 molecular changes*) and a fragment (*most of which had never been associated with exercise*).

### 39. A: Combining sentences

If you're not sure about A initially, leave it. B and C are incorrect because they create comma splices. When used at the start of a clause, *consequently* and *therefore* should only follow a period or semicolon, not a comma. In D, the gerund *occurring* creates a fragment. That leaves A, which correctly places a comma between a complete sentence (*It works by setting off a chemical reaction that "tricks" cells into thinking they need energy*) and a fragment (*thereby increasing their metabolism*). Although *thereby* may sound strange to you, it is a synonym for *therefore* and is perfectly acceptable.

### 40. B: Dangling modifier

Who consumed a single dose? The mice. So *the mice*, the subject, must appear immediately after the comma. Since that is not the case, A can be eliminated. In order to correct the error, the subject must appear in the first clause. B is the only option to include *the mice*.

### 41. C: Graphic

The question actually gives you an important piece of information: it tells you that the correct answer must support the main topic of the paragraph. If you know what that topic is, you can narrow down the answers before you even look at the graph. What is the point of the paragraph? Compound 14 helped mice lose weight. It is thus logical to assume that the mice receiving Compound 14 lost more weight than the mice not receiving the compound. B can therefore be eliminated. Now look at the graph: the line for the inactive compound rises, indicating that that group of mice gained weight, while the line for the active compound dips, indicating that that group lost weight. The numbers 1-7 represent days; they have nothing to do with how much weight was lost or gained. A can therefore be eliminated. C and D both correctly indicate that the Compound 14 mice lost about 2 grams, so focus on the line for the other group: it ends up somewhere between 1 and 2, so those mice gained more than one gram but less than 2. C is therefore correct.

### 42. A: Pronoun agreement, apostrophes

Start with the pronoun. *It's* must logically refer to Compound 14 (singular). The singular pronoun is therefore correct, eliminating D. Since you wouldn't say "…and analyze it is long term effects," you need the possessive *its* (= the effects of Compound 14). That eliminates C. Now look at the noun: there's no noun after *effects*, so it must be plural. Since plural nouns do not take apostrophes, B can be eliminated. That leaves A, which provides the correct noun and pronoun.

### 43. A: Add/delete/change

What is the focus of the sentence? The huge number of people who suffer from obesity and diabetes. What is the focus of the paragraph? The potential benefits of Compound 14 for people with obesity and diabetes. Are those ideas similar or different? Similar. So the sentence should be added. The sentence says nothing about Compound 14's long-term effects, so B can be eliminated. C correctly indicates that the statistics in the sentence clarify precisely what is meant by *widespread* (previous sentence).

## 44. D: Non-essential vs. essential clause

Since the original version contains two commas, indicating a non-essential clause, cross out the clause and read the sentence without it: *Researchers also believe that exercise pills could strongly benefit people…as well as those born with physical limitations*. Even though the sentence still makes grammatical sense, it no longer makes logical sense. The sentence is not referring to people in general but rather to a specific group of people: those born with physical limitations. The clause is therefore essential, and no commas should be used.

# Test 6 Answer Sheet

1. Ⓐ Ⓑ Ⓒ Ⓓ
2. Ⓐ Ⓑ Ⓒ Ⓓ
3. Ⓐ Ⓑ Ⓒ Ⓓ
4. Ⓐ Ⓑ Ⓒ Ⓓ
5. Ⓐ Ⓑ Ⓒ Ⓓ
6. Ⓐ Ⓑ Ⓒ Ⓓ
7. Ⓐ Ⓑ Ⓒ Ⓓ
8. Ⓐ Ⓑ Ⓒ Ⓓ
9. Ⓐ Ⓑ Ⓒ Ⓓ
10. Ⓐ Ⓑ Ⓒ Ⓓ
11. Ⓐ Ⓑ Ⓒ Ⓓ
12. Ⓐ Ⓑ Ⓒ Ⓓ
13. Ⓐ Ⓑ Ⓒ Ⓓ
14. Ⓐ Ⓑ Ⓒ Ⓓ
15. Ⓐ Ⓑ Ⓒ Ⓓ
16. Ⓐ Ⓑ Ⓒ Ⓓ
17. Ⓐ Ⓑ Ⓒ Ⓓ
18. Ⓐ Ⓑ Ⓒ Ⓓ
19. Ⓐ Ⓑ Ⓒ Ⓓ
20. Ⓐ Ⓑ Ⓒ Ⓓ
21. Ⓐ Ⓑ Ⓒ Ⓓ
22. Ⓐ Ⓑ Ⓒ Ⓓ

23. Ⓐ Ⓑ Ⓒ Ⓓ
24. Ⓐ Ⓑ Ⓒ Ⓓ
25. Ⓐ Ⓑ Ⓒ Ⓓ
26. Ⓐ Ⓑ Ⓒ Ⓓ
27. Ⓐ Ⓑ Ⓒ Ⓓ
28. Ⓐ Ⓑ Ⓒ Ⓓ
29. Ⓐ Ⓑ Ⓒ Ⓓ
30. Ⓐ Ⓑ Ⓒ Ⓓ
31. Ⓐ Ⓑ Ⓒ Ⓓ
32. Ⓐ Ⓑ Ⓒ Ⓓ
33. Ⓐ Ⓑ Ⓒ Ⓓ
34. Ⓐ Ⓑ Ⓒ Ⓓ
35. Ⓐ Ⓑ Ⓒ Ⓓ
36. Ⓐ Ⓑ Ⓒ Ⓓ
37. Ⓐ Ⓑ Ⓒ Ⓓ
38. Ⓐ Ⓑ Ⓒ Ⓓ
39. Ⓐ Ⓑ Ⓒ Ⓓ
40. Ⓐ Ⓑ Ⓒ Ⓓ
41. Ⓐ Ⓑ Ⓒ Ⓓ
42. Ⓐ Ⓑ Ⓒ Ⓓ
43. Ⓐ Ⓑ Ⓒ Ⓓ
44. Ⓐ Ⓑ Ⓒ Ⓓ

# Writing and Language Test
## 35 MINUTES, 44 QUESTIONS

**Turn to Section 2 of your answer sheet to answer the questions in this section.**

### DIRECTIONS

Each passage below is accompanied by a number of questions. For some questions, you will consider how the passage might be revised to improve the expression of ideas. For other questions, you will consider how the passage might be edited to correct errors in sentence structure, usage, or punctuation. A passage or a question may be accompanied by one or more graphics (such as a table or graph) that you will consider as you make revising and editing decisions.

Some questions will direct you to an underlined portion of a passage. Other questions will direct you to a location in a passage or ask you to think about the passage as a whole.

After reading each passage, choose the answer to each question that most effectively improves the quality of writing in the passage or that makes the passage conform to the conventions of standard written English. Many questions include a "NO CHANGE" option. Choose that option if you think the best choice is to leave the relevant portion of the passage as it is.

**Questions 1-11 are based on the following passage and supplemental information.**

**The Great Race**

You can't compare it to any other competitive event in the world. A race over 1150 miles of the roughest, most beautiful terrain that nature has to offer, the Iditarod **[1]** includes: jagged mountain ranges, frozen rivers, dense forest, desolate tundra, and miles of windswept coast. **[2]** Adding temperatures far below zero, winds that can cause a complete loss of visibility, and treacherous climbs, and you have an extraordinary event – one that is only possible in Alaska.

**1**
A) NO CHANGE
B) includes jagged mountain ranges; frozen rivers; dense forest,
C) includes; jagged mountain ranges, frozen rivers, dense forest
D) includes jagged mountain ranges, frozen rivers, dense forest,

**2**
A) NO CHANGE
B) To add
C) If you add
D) Add

From Anchorage in south central Alaska to Nome on the western Bering Sea coast, each team of 12 to 16 dogs and their driver – known as a musher – **3** cover over a thousand miles in 10 to 17 days. Journalists from outdoor magazines, adventure magazines, and newspapers flock to Anchorage and Nome to record the excitement. **4** With more than 250,000 residents, Anchorage is a vibrant, modern city. The atmosphere is festive, with volunteers milling around to support the mushers and their families and coordinate supplies.

**3**

A) NO CHANGE
B) covers
C) have covered
D) covering

**4**

The writer is considering deleting the underlined sentence. Should it be kept or deleted?

A) Kept, because it provides a relevant description of the Iditarod's starting location.
B) Kept, because it explains why many journalists gather in Anchorage.
C) Deleted, because it suggests that most Alaskan cities lack modern conveniences.
D) Deleted, because the description of Anchorage is irrelevant to the focus of the paragraph.

Usually, a few mushers are full-time professional athletes, but the majority work in other fields. Some races, **5** however, have included mushers who were lawyers, miners, and artists. Professional or not, the mushers must spend months training with their dogs – but the reward for winning is great. Every year, the top mushers and their dogs become local celebrities. **6** Racing associations are even working toward making mushing an Olympic sport. This popularity is credited with the resurgence of recreational mushing in Alaska over the last few decades. Of the fifty or so mushers who enter the race each year, the majority reside in Alaska year-round; however, competitors from fourteen countries have successfully competed in the event. **7**

**5**

A) NO CHANGE
B) for example,
C) on the other hand,
D) moreover,

**6**

Which choice most logically follows the previous sentence?

A) NO CHANGE
B) Sled dogs are intelligent, intuitive, and able to find trails in difficult conditions.
C) The teams are profiled in newspapers and interviewed on television.
D) Although dogsled racing receives more publicity, recreational mushing thrives as an unorganized sport.

**7**

At this point, the writer is considering adding the following sentence.

In 1992, Switzerland's Martin Buser became the first international winner.

Should the writer make this addition?

A) Yes, because it supports the point that most mushers are not professional athletes.
B) Yes, because it provides a specific illustration of the claim made in the previous sentence.
C) No, because it implies that Alaskan mushers can no longer compete successfully.
D) No, because it is inconsistent with the paragraph's focus on recreational musing.

From the starting line in Anchorage, the dog teams run to the first checkpoint at Eagle River. The mushers then leave the land of highways and modern conveniences and head up through Finger Lake to a river **8** highway. They are taken west through the arctic tundra. Finally, the exhausted teams arrive at the coast and ride into Nome, where **9** they give the mushers and dogs a hero's welcome.

The Iditarod is a commemoration of a not-so-distant past that Alaskans take pride in. The Iditarod Trail, which is today recognized as a national landmark by the National Historical **10** Registry, but it began as a mail and supply route. In 1925, part of the trail became a life-saving highway. A Diphtheria epidemic threatened the population of Nome, and intrepid mushers and their faithful dogs fought their way through the untamed wilderness to bring life-saving medication. Today, the running of the Iditarod is an annual commemoration of that **11** triumph.

**8**

What is the best way to combine the sentences at the underlined portion?

A) highway that takes them west
B) highway, it takes them west
C) highway and taken west
D) highway, and they are taken west by this

**9**

A) NO CHANGE
B) a hero's welcome being given to the mushers and dogs.
C) the mushers and dogs are given a hero's welcome.
D) the giving of a hero's welcome to the mushers and dogs occurs.

**10**

A) NO CHANGE
B) Registry, and it
C) Registry, so it
D) Registry,

**11**

A) NO CHANGE
B) prediction.
C) problem.
D) exploration.

## Questions 12-22 are based on the following passage.

### Reusable Rocket

Everything about space flight is exaggerated; even the smallest rockets are hundreds of feet high. The largest rocket ever built – the Saturn V, which launched the first space station and sent astronauts to the **12** Moon, remaining the most powerful vehicle in history. But the cost of space flight is exaggerated, too. **13** As a result of their technological sophistication, rockets are one-shot wonders. **14** After firing their engines for only a few minutes, they fall back to Earth, where they usually splash unseen into the ocean.

Rocket scientists have long dreamed of building a rocket capable of flying multiple missions. Such a **15** machine, they hope, would reduce the price of traveling into space. The only multi-missions rocket built so far proved to be a dangerous and expensive disappointment that far exceeded the budget its designers had intended.

**12**

A) NO CHANGE
B) Moon; it remains
C) Moon – remains
D) Moon, remain

**13**

A) NO CHANGE
B) Despite
C) Before
D) In addition to

**14**

Which choice most logically follows the previous sentence?

A) NO CHANGE
B) Rockets built in the future will be long and thin, more closely resembling the first rockets than the ones built today.
C) Unlike a jet engine, which requires air to work, a rocket ship needs only fuel to function.
D) In contrast, some space crafts such as satellites are built to enter into orbit rather than return to Earth.

**15**

A) NO CHANGE
B) machine, it is their hope
C) machine, they hope
D) machine in the hope

Airbus, which leads the production of the Ariane rocket, has developed a concept that could lead to recyclable space vehicles. Code-named "Adeline," the system would allow a booster's main engines to fly **16** itself back to Earth after a launch.

The Adeline rocket is only partially reusable, but it's intended to **17** do some pretty awesome stuff. It would consist **18** in an upper section, which contained the fuselage and propellant tanks, and a lower module that housed the main engine – the most expensive (and arguably the most important) part of the rocket. The lower module would play a key role in lifting the rocket off the **19** launch pad once the propellants in the upper tanks were exhausted, however, the module would detach itself from the upper part of the rocket and return to Earth.

**16**

A) NO CHANGE
B) oneself
C) him- or herself
D) themselves

**17**

Which choice is most consistent with the tone established in the passage?

A) NO CHANGE
B) demonstrate an ingenious functionality.
C) function in a very creative manner.
D) work in a really cool way.

**18**

A) NO CHANGE
B) for
C) on
D) of

**19**

A) NO CHANGE
B) launch pad. Once the propellants in the upper tanks were exhausted,
C) launch pad, once the propellants in the upper tanks were exhausted
D) launch pad once the propellants, in the upper tanks were exhausted,

[1] The next step would be re-entry into the Earth's atmosphere. [2] **20** Communicating with satellite operators and government space stations, the module would have a heat shield on its bulbous nose. [3] At a certain point in the descent, the module would pull up using its small winglets and steer itself towards a runway. [4] The recovered engines could then be readied for the next launch. [5] Drone technology would help it stay on course, and wings as well as small, deployable propellers would allow it to touch down gently like a small plane. **21**

If the Adeline project is successful, its technology could transform the space industry. Engines could be re-flown between 10 and 20 times, allowing about 80% of the rocket's economic value to be recovered. Airbus engineers believe that the basic concept could be incorporated into any liquid-fuelled rocket, however large or small. Someday, perhaps, **22** rocket travel will be as common as airplane travel is today.

**20**

Which choice provides the most logical introduction to the sentence?

A) NO CHANGE
B) Having traveled thousands of miles,
C) To protect against extreme temperatures,
D) Heading toward an airport in French Guyana,

**21**

The best placement for sentence 4 is

A) where it is now.
B) after sentence 1.
C) after sentence 2.
D) after sentence 5.

**22**

A) NO CHANGE
B) travel by rocket ship will be as common as traveling in an airplane today.
C) travel by rocket ship will be as common as airplanes are today.
D) rocket travel will be as common as when you travel by airplane today.

**Questions 23-33 are based on the following passage.**

**Maxine Hong Kingston**

As the daughter of Chinese immigrants, Maxine Hong Kingston **23** enjoyed learning about traditions from a wide variety of cultures. She watched her parents' attempts to assimilate into American life, but she also listened intently to their tales of the country they had left behind. **24** She was entranced by Chinese folk tales and stories about her ancestors. She also discovered that her family had faced many difficulties in China.

**23**

Which choice provides the most effective introduction to the passage?

A) NO CHANGE
B) always felt the pull of two cultures.
C) has received several awards for her contributions to Chinese-American literature.
D) majored in English at the University of California, Berkeley.

**24**

What is the most effective way of combining the underlined sentences?

A) While she was entranced by Chinese folk tales and stories about her ancestors, she also discovered that her family had faced many difficulties in China.

B) Entranced by Chinese folk tales and stories about her ancestors, the discovery was made by her that her family had faced many difficulties in China.

C) She was entranced by traditional Chinese folk tales and stories about her ancestors; therefore, she discovered that her family had faced many difficulties in China.

D) She was entranced by traditional Chinese folk tales and stories about her ancestors, and, moreover, discovered that many difficulties had been faced by her family in China.

As an adult, Kingston came to view her writing as a means of reconciling the two sides of her identity and **25** to understand the adversity her relatives had encountered in their homeland. Blending fiction and autobiography, myth and realism, **26** elements of both Chinese and the American literary traditions are incorporated into her books.

　　The author of seven novels and two anthologies, Kingston always believed that she was born to be a writer. **27** As a small child, she delighted in making up her own stories and narrating them to her parents. When she learned to write, she immediately began to record the tales her mother told her. It was, she says, as if writing had chosen her.

　　Kingston did not become a professional writer immediately, though. After graduating from the University of California at Berkeley, she worked as a high school teacher for more than a decade. Finally, in 1976, she published her first book, *The Woman Warrior: Memoirs of a Girlhood Among Ghosts*. The book, which explored the lives of the women **28** whom had most strongly influenced Kingston, was both a novel and a memoir, and it earned Kingston immediate critical acclaim.

**25**

A) NO CHANGE
B) she understands
C) understanding
D) understood

**26**

A) NO CHANGE
B) elements of both Chinese and American literary traditions being incorporated into Kingston's books.
C) the incorporation of elements of both Chinese and American literary traditions can be seen in Kingston's books.
D) Kingston's books incorporate elements of both Chinese and American literary traditions.

**27**

The writer is considering the deleting the underlined sentence. Should it be kept or deleted?

A) Kept, because it supports the idea that Kingston was drawn to writing early in her life.
B) Kept, because it explains why Kingston wrote her novels in English rather than Chinese.
C) Deleted, because it repeats information presented earlier in the passage.
D) Deleted, because it blurs the passage's focus on Kingston's adult writing.

**28**

A) NO CHANGE
B) who
C) which
D) they

Kingston wrote her second book, *China Men*, as a tribute to her father and male relatives. In that work, she **29** copies the stories of a group of men who leave China to settle in the United States, following their families for several generations. The characters include Kingston's father, BaBa, a Laundromat owner; her grandfather Ah Goong, a railroad worker; and her great-grandfather, **30** Bak Goong, who farmed sugar on a plantation in Hawaii.

**31** Though Kingston's work has generally earned praise from reviewers, it has also received some criticism. Although Kingston based the characters on members of her own family, some of the book's more dramatic incidents are products of **32** its imagination. Kingston did, however, find a way to incorporate her father directly into the book. For the Chinese translation of *China Men*, she asked him to provide his own commentary in the margins of each page – a classical Chinese technique. She considers that edition one of her highest achievements **33** while it allowed her to honor her father for his writing as well as his personal accomplishments.

**29**

A) NO CHANGE
B) traces
C) engraves
D) shades

**30**

Which choice most effectively preserves the sentence pattern established in the paragraph?

A) NO CHANGE
B) Bak Goong, who worked on a plantation in Hawaii farming sugar.
C) Bak Goong, who worked in Hawaii on a plantation farming sugar.
D) Bak Goong, a sugar farmer on a plantation in Hawaii.

**31**

Which choice most logically sets up the information that follows?

A) NO CHANGE
B) Kingston wrote *The Woman Warrior* and *China Men* as a single novel.
C) Like Kingston's other novels, *China Men* is a combination of fact and fiction.
D) In 1990, filmmaker Gayle K. Yamada released a documentary about Kingston's work.

**32**

A) NO CHANGE
B) their
C) they're
D) her

**33**

A) NO CHANGE
B) because
C) although
D) until

**Questions 34-44 are based on the following passage.**

**Summer Intern**

Over the past few years, I've held a variety of summer 34 jobs. Camp counselor, ice cream-scooper, and dog walker, to name just a few. Last summer, however, I wanted to gain experience applying my coursework in Marketing to a real-world office environment. I wasn't sure how to go about finding an 35 internship, but I visited my college's career office.

As I learned from speaking to a counselor and 36 independently doing internet research on my own, internships vary greatly depending on work, time, and compensation. Most school-year internships require a commitment of about 10 to 15 hours, whereas summer internships can involve up to 40 hours a week. 37 While the majority of paid internships lead to a job offer, only a small percentage of unpaid internships lead to permanent positions.

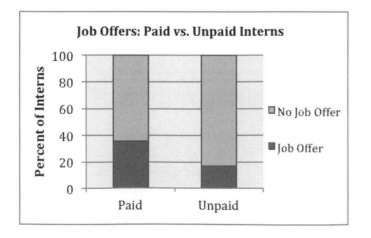

**34**

A) NO CHANGE
B) jobs, camp counselor,
C) jobs: camp counselor,
D) jobs; camp counselor,

**35**

A) NO CHANGE
B) internship, so
C) internship, and
D) internship, therefore

**36**

A) NO CHANGE
B) doing independent internet research on my own,
C) independently researching on my own,
D) doing independent research,

**37**

Which choice most accurately describes the data in the graph?

A) NO CHANGE
B) While a small percentage of paid internships lead to a job offer, a much higher percentage of unpaid internships lead to permanent positions.
C) Both paid and unpaid interns have an excellent chance of obtaining permanent employment through their internship.
D) While most internships do not lead to permanent positions, paid internships are more likely to lead to permanent jobs than are unpaid internships.

[38] I identified some local businesses that were advertising for student interns, I emailed their hiring managers with a statement of interest and my resume. I had read that competition for internships can be very [39] rigid, so I was surprised to receive several phone calls immediately. After several interviews, I was offered a full-time sales and marketing internship at a local startup company. Since this was my first real professional experience, I wasn't sure what to expect.

**38**

A) NO CHANGE
B) I had identified
C) Being that I had identified
D) Having identified

**39**

A) NO CHANGE
B) stiff,
C) fixed,
D) taut,

As I discovered, my job changed on an almost daily basis. Because the company was so new, employees' roles being fluid: workers devoted time to the [40] projects, that required the most help, regardless of their official titles. I did everything from conducting market research to designing surveys to managing social media accounts. [41] Some days I left at 3 o'clock, but other times I worked late into the night. Likewise, my assignments ranged in length from a few hours to a few weeks. Every day was different, and I was almost never bored. While I was initially hesitant to ask my coworkers for help, I quickly learned that they were eager to share their insights with me. [42] Moreover, I realized that everyone in the office [43] has an important role to play. With even one person missing, the team could not function effectively.

**40**

A) NO CHANGE
B) projects that,
C) projects that
D) projects, which

**41**

At this point, the writer is considering adding the following sentence.

　　My schedule was similarly unpredictable.

Should the writer make this addition?

A) Yes, because it explains why the writer was able to leave early some days.
B) Yes, because it effectively sets up the examples that follow.
C) No, because it is irrelevant to the description of the projects the writer worked on.
D) No, because it detracts from the paragraph's focus on the writer's coworkers.

**42**

A) NO CHANGE
B) However,
C) Granted,
D) Therefore,

**43**

A) NO CHANGE
B) has had
C) would have
D) had

The opportunity to contribute to such an exciting, fast-paced environment made me aware of the possibilities that await me after graduation. My internship changed my perspective and pushed me to discover new strengths and abilities. **44** Almost anyone can find an internship that suits his or her particular interests.

**44**

Which choice most logically concludes the passage while reinforcing its main theme?

A) NO CHANGE

B) I intend to stay in contact with some of my colleagues during the school year.

C) I wouldn't have traded it for a traditional 9-5 experience, and I'm already making plans to return next summer.

D) Not all internships are created equal; some positions are really just part-time temporary jobs.

**Test 6: Explanations**

1. D: Colon, commas with list

A colon should only be used after a complete, standalone sentence, and the phrase before the colon cannot stand on its own (*A race over 1150 miles of the roughest, most beautiful terrain that nature has to offer, the Iditarod includes*). That eliminates A. B is incorrect because either commas or semicolons should be used between the items in a list; they should not be mixed and matched. C is incorrect because a semicolon should not be used before a list. That leaves D, which correctly eliminates the colon and places a comma between each of the items in the list.

2. D: Sentence vs. fragment

If you can't answer this question by ear, you can think of it grammatically. The construction "comma + and" later in the sentence is the grammatical equivalent of a period – it indicates that a complete sentence must appear both before and after. The only part you need to worry about is the statement before "comma + and:" *Adding temperatures far below zero, winds that can cause a complete loss of visibility, and treacherous climbs*. That's not a complete sentence, so your job is to make it into one. A clause that begins with *if* cannot stand alone as a complete sentence, so C can be eliminated. Now, think of it this way: although the non-underlined portion of the statement contains a list with verbs, it doesn't contain a *main* verb. A main verb must be conjugated, so the gerund *adding* doesn't work. Neither does the infinitive *to add*. That leaves D. In this case, the verb *add* is a command, so the subject (you) is implied.

3. B: Subject-verb agreement

The subject of the underlined verb is *each team*, which is singular. A singular verb (*covers*) is therefore required.

4. D: Add/delete/change

What is the focus of the sentence? The fact that Anchorage is a large, modern city. What is the paragraph about? The amount of terrain the

mushers cover, and the press coverage the Iditarod attracts. Are those ideas similar or different? Different. So the sentence should not be added because it is off-topic. That makes the answer D.

5. B: Transition

Remember that when a transition is used non-essentially (between commas), it is usually indicating a relationship between the sentence in which it appears and the previous sentence. Sentence 1: Mushers work in many different fields. Sentence 2: Mushers have been lawyers, miners, etc. Logically, the second sentence is giving examples of the kinds of careers former mushers have had. B is therefore the only possibility.

6. C: Add/delete/change

What is the focus of the previous sentence? Mushers become local celebrities. Only B is consistent with that ideas – being profiled in newspapers and appearing on television are things that local celebrities do. The other answers are related to the Iditarod/dogsled racing but do not logically follow from the previous sentence.

7. B: Add/delete/change

What is the focus of the sentence? The first international Iditarod winner. What is the focus of the paragraph? The mushers' backgrounds and popularity? Does it fit? Maybe. To check it out, look at the previous sentence – the sentence to be added must logically follow that sentence. In this case, the previous sentence introduces the idea that successful competitors have come from outside the United States. In that context, Buser is clearly an example of a successful international (Swiss) competitor. The sentence should therefore be added, and the answer is B.

8. A: Combining sentences

You can assume that B and D are incorrect right away: B contains the construction "comma + it," which normally signals a comma splice, and D is noticeably longer than the other answers. It also contains the word *this* without a noun after it –

another sign of a wrong answer. Plug A into the sentence: *The mushers then leave the land of highways and modern conveniences and head up through Finger Lake to a river highway that takes them west through the arctic tundra*. Yes, that makes sense. If you're not sure, though, check C: *The mushers then leave the land of highways and modern conveniences and head up through Finger Lake to a river highway and taken west through the arctic tundra*. No. In addition to creating an awkward construction by repeating the word *and*, this option is missing a word: the mushers *are taken*. A is therefore correct.

9. C: Pronoun agreement

Because the "teams" include mushers, the word *they* cannot refer to the mushers. Rather, it must refer to the people greeting the mushers. Because the sentence does not actually mention those people anywhere, the pronoun is missing a referent. A is therefore incorrect. B is incorrect because the gerund *being* creates a fragment, and D is incorrect because it contains a wordy and awkward construction. C creates a clean, concise construction that removes the pronoun agreement problem by eliminating the pronoun.

10. D: Non-essential clause

The fastest way to answer this question is to recognize that "comma + and, but, and so" = period. Plug in a period and read the sentence from the beginning: *The Iditarod Trail, which is today recognized as a national landmark by the National Historical Registry. It began as a mail and supply route.* The first "sentence" is actually a fragment, so A, B, and C can be eliminated. Alternately, you can recognize that the comma before *which* earlier in the sentence marks the start of a non-essential clause. If you cross out the clause, you get this: *The Iditarod Trail … but it began as a mail and supply route.* Clearly, that doesn't make sense. The easiest way to turn that statement into a sentence is to remove the transition + *it*. Again, that makes D the answer.

11. A: Diction

The underlined noun refers to the situation described in the previous sentence, namely that mushers and their dogs brought life-saving serum to the Nome residents suffering from diphtheria. That's a good thing, so C can be eliminated. It's also not a prediction or an exploration (the mushers had a specific destination). That leaves *triumph*, which is consistent with the mushers' successful delivery of the serum.

12. C: Dash, non-essential clause

If you look earlier in the sentence, you'll see a dash. Dashes go with dashes, so you can assume the answer is C. When you plug it in, you get this: *The largest rocket ever built – the Saturn V, which launched the first space station and sent astronauts to the Moon – remains the most powerful vehicle in history.* When the non-essential clause is removed, the sentence still makes perfect grammatical sense, indicating that the answer is in fact C.

13. B: Transition

The two parts of the sentence express opposing ideas (rockets are sophisticated vs. rockets can only be used once), so a contradictor is required. *Despite* is the only contradictor, so the original version is correct.

14. A: Add/delete/change

What does the previous sentence indicate? Rockets can only be used once. The original version is most consistent with that idea, as indicated by the phrase *for only a few minutes*. The other options are related to space travel but do not logically follow from the previous sentence.

15. A: Non-essential clause

The commas around *they hope* indicate that this phrase can be crossed out of the sentence. When it is crossed out, the sentence still makes grammatical sense: *Such a machine…would reduce the price of traveling into space.* As a result, the commas are correct. Although the placement of the non-essential clause may seem odd to you, this construction is perfectly acceptable.

### 16. D: Pronoun agreement

Logically, the underlined pronoun must refer to the plural noun *the main engines* (what else could fly itself back to Earth?). *Itself* is singular, eliminating A. *Oneself* and *him- or herself* are singular but only refer to people. *Themselves* is plural and correctly refers to things.

### 17. C: Register

The original version and D are both far too informal, and B is too formal. Only C is consistent with the passage's straightforward, moderately serious style.

### 18. D: Preposition, idiom

The correct idiom is "consist of." A preposition other than *of* should not be used.

### 19. B: Separating sentences

If you read the sentence from the beginning and notice that there are actually two sentences, you can jump right to B since that is the only option to include a period or a semicolon. (As a general rule, you should check options involving periods first.) Otherwise, the key to answering this question is to recognize that although the phrase *once the propellants in the upper tanks were exhausted* appears to belong to the end of the first sentence, it also makes sense as the beginning of the second sentence. C is incorrect because the comma before *once* creates a comma splice, and D is incorrect because it fails to put any punctuation between the two sentences.

### 20. C: Add/delete/change

What does the second half of the sentence indicate? The module would have a heat shield. Why would it have a heat shield? Because it would be exposed to very high heat. C is the only answer consistent with that idea.

### 21. D: Sentence order

What is the focus of sentence 4? The fact that the engines could be reused, presumably after their return. Since the paragraph focuses on the process by which the engines would return, sentence 4 most logically belongs at the end. Indeed, sentence 5 describes the landing – since the engines could only be re-launched after landing, sentence 4 must come after sentence 5.

### 22. A: Faulty comparison

The original version correctly uses a parallel construction to compare rocket travel to airplane travel. All of the other options compare unalike items or contain non-parallel constructions.

### 23. B: Add/delete/change

Although the question asks about the passage as a whole, you only need to read the rest of the introduction to answer the question. It describes the tension between China and America that Kingston felt growing up. The answer most consistent with that idea is B. Careful with A: Kingston clearly was interested in learning about "traditions," but the passage only discusses China and America – there is nothing about other cultures. C and D provide biographical information that does not relate to the passage as a whole.

### 24. A: Combining sentences

Because the first sentence contains a positive idea (*entranced by folktales*) whereas the second sentence contains a negative one (*faced many difficulties*), a contradictor is required. A is the only option to contain a contradictor (*while*). *Therefore* in C and *moreover* in D are both continuers. Although the sentence could also be written without a transition, B contains a dangling modifier. The phrase *Entranced by Chinese folk tales and stories about her ancestors* must logically describe *her*, the subject, but that word does not appear immediately after the comma.

### 25. C: Parallel structure

The word *and* pairs the underlined verb with *reconciling*, so the correct answer must end in -ING as well. That makes C the only option.

**26. D: Dangling modifier**

What blends fiction and autobiography, myth and realism? Kingston's books. So *Kingston's books*, the subject, must appear immediately after the comma. The only answer to contain that construction is D.

**27. A: Add/delete/change**

What is the focus of the underlined sentence? Kingston liked to make up stories as a child. What is the focus of the paragraph? Kingston felt that she was born to be a writer. Are those ideas similar or different? Similar. So the sentence should be kept. A is correct because the underlined sentence builds logically on the statement in the previous sentence. It has nothing to do with explaining Kingston's choice of language, eliminating B.

**28. B: Who vs. whom**

*Who*, not *whom*, should not come before a verb (*had*). That eliminates A and makes B correct. *Which* is for things, eliminating C, and *they* creates a nonsense construction, eliminating D.

**29. B: Diction**

*Trace a story* is an idiom meaning "follow the course of a story." The other options are related to (literal) tracing but do not have the same idiomatic definition.

**30. D: Parallel structure**

Each of the other items in the list contains the construction *Name, a _____*, so the third item must match. Only D contains the correct construction.

**31. C: Add/delete/change**

What is the focus of the information that follows? Kingston's books are based on both real people and events she imagined. The phrase *a combination of fact and fiction* in C is most consistent with that idea. The other answers are off-topic.

**32. D: Pronoun agreement**

Logically, the underlined pronoun must refer to Kingston; *its* could only refer to the book, and books don't have imaginations. *Her* is therefore the only possible answer.

**33. B: Transition**

Logically, the first part of the sentence is the result of the second: Kingston considered the Chinese translation of *China Men* among her highest achievements <u>because</u> it allowed her to honor her father. *While* and *although* are contradictors and do not fit logically, and *until* makes no sense at all in context since the sentence has nothing to do with time.

**34. C: Colon**

A period and a semicolon are grammatically identical, so both A and D can be eliminated immediately. A comma should not be used to introduce a list, eliminating B. C correctly uses a colon to introduce a list.

**35. B: Transition**

Logically, the second half of the sentence is the result of the first: the writer visited the career office because he/she didn't know how to go about finding an internship. That eliminates A and C. Although *so* and *therefore* are synonyms, *so* follows a comma whereas *therefore* follows a semicolon or period. That eliminates D and makes B correct.

**36. D: Redundancy, shorter is better**

*Independently* and *on my own* have the same meaning, so only one of these options should be used.

**37. D: Graphic**

The chart shows two stacked bars: one for paid and one for unpaid interns. The most important thing to recognize is that for both paid and unpaid interns, the light gray bay (no job offer) is much longer than the dark gray bar (job offer). That means most internships, both paid and unpaid, do not lead to a job offer. The statement that *the majority of internships lead to a job offer* is therefore false, eliminating A. C can likewise be eliminated because neither paid nor unpaid interns have an "excellent" chance of receiving a job offer. Be careful with B: it states exactly the opposite of what the graph shows. *Paid* internships lead to job offers at a much higher rate (approximately 20 percentage points) than unpaid internships. D correctly states that fact.

38. D: Comma splice

If you just read the beginning of the sentence, you're likely to think the original version is fine; however, the construction "comma + I" later in the sentence signals a comma splice. Since a comma can only be placed between a dependent clause (fragment) and an independent clause (sentence), it is necessary to make the first clause dependent. B creates the same problem as A. In C, the phrase *being that* is awkward and creates an illogical relationship (the second clause is not the result of the first). D is correct because the replacement of the subject and verb with *having* makes the first clause dependent and eliminates the comma splice.

39. B: Idiom

The correct idiom is "stiff competition." The other adjectives are not idiomatic.

40. C: Essential vs. non-essential clause

Since a comma should not come before or after *that*, A and B can be eliminated immediately. D is incorrect because the comma before *which* would create a non-essential clause (*which required the most help*). Although the sentence would still make grammatical sense if the clause were removed (*workers devoted time to the projects … regardless of their titles*), it would no longer make logical sense because we wouldn't know which projects were being referred to. The information is therefore essential, making the answer C.

41. B: Add/delete/change

What is the focus of the sentence? The writer's schedule was unpredictable. What is the focus of the paragraph? The writer's job changed a lot. Are those ideas similar or different. Similar. That eliminates C and D. Be careful with A: the sentence itself does not actually *explain* why the writer was able to leave early some days – it's simply consistent with that idea. B is correct because the sentence to be inserted (general) sets up the specific example of *how* the writer's schedule varied.

42. A: Transition

Start by crossing out the original transition and considering the relationship between the sentence in question and the previous question. Sentence 1: My coworkers were happy to share their knowledge with me. Sentence 2: I learned that everyone had something to contribute. Those are similar ideas, so a continuer is required. That eliminates B and C (*granted* is used to introduce a concession – a recognition that an opposing idea has some merit). The second sentence is not the result of the first, so *therefore* does not fit. That leaves *moreover*, which correctly indicates that the second sentences continues in the same direction as the first.

43. D: Tense

The surrounding verbs (*was*, *learned*, *realized*) are all in the past tense, so the underlined verb should be in the past as well. Only *had* is in the correct tense. *Has had* (present perfect), *has* (present), and *would have* (conditional) all do not fit.

44. C: Add/delete/change

What is the focus of the passage? Basically, how much the writer enjoyed and learned from his or her internship. Logically, then, the conclusion should be consistent with that idea and be written in the first person. Only B and C contain the word *I*, so you can assume one of those is correct. B is positive but too specific; it doesn't fit with the passage as a whole. C is much more general and is therefore a more effective conclusion.

# ABOUT THE AUTHOR

Erica Meltzer has worked as a tutor, test-prep writer, and blogger since 2007. In addition to *The Ultimate Guide to SAT Grammar*, she is the author of *The Critical Reader*, *The Complete Guide to ACT English*, and *The Complete Guide to ACT Reading*. Her books are used by tutors and tutoring companies both in the United States and around the world. She lives in New York City, and you can visit her online at www.thecriticalreader.com.